# Junior Great Books

SERIES 6

FIRST SEMESTER

◆ ◆ ◆

AN INTERPRETIVE READING, WRITING,

AND DISCUSSION CURRICULUM

# JUNIOR GREAT BOOKS

SERIES 6                    FIRST SEMESTER

THE GREAT BOOKS FOUNDATION

*A nonprofit educational corporation*

First Printing

9    8

Printed in the United States of America

Published and distributed by

THE GREAT BOOKS FOUNDATION
*A nonprofit educational corporation*

35 East Wacker Drive, Suite 2300

Chicago, IL 60601-2298

# CONTENTS

# PREFACE

## SHARED INQUIRY

In Junior Great Books you will explore a number of outstanding stories. You will do this in a variety of ways: by taking notes as you read, by looking at important words and passages, and by sharing your questions and ideas about each story with your group. In each of these activities, you and your classmates will be working together with your teacher or leader, asking and answering questions about what the story means. You will be sharing what you discover with your classmates. This way of reading, writing, and discussion in Junior Great Books is called *shared inquiry.*

One of the good things about shared inquiry is that you can speak without worrying about whether what you say is "the right answer." Different ideas and points of view can all lead to a better understanding of the story. When you speak, the leader may ask you to back up what you have said, or urge you to develop your idea further. Others in your class may also respond to what you say. They, too, may be asked to support their statements or explain them more clearly. After listening to what others say, you may change your mind about your answer. Shared inquiry gives you the chance to learn both from the author and from one another.

Sometimes you will focus on a small part of the story; at other times, you will think about the story as a whole.

Whether you are working on your own or with others, in shared inquiry you will develop *interpretations* of what you read—you will be working to discover what the author wants to tell you or make you feel through his or her words.

## WHAT IS INTERPRETATION?

Good writers do their work with care. There are reasons for everything they put into their stories. They try to include only what has a point and what fits—things needed to make a story clear, to make it interesting, and to keep it moving along. They waste few words. In really good stories, everything fits. Everything has an explanation. The parts are connected and support one another just as the posts and beams in a building do.

The parts of the story, because they are connected, help to explain one another. Authors do not point out exactly how the parts are connected, nor do they say in so many words why everything in a story happens as it does. For one thing, that would make the story dull. For another, they want stories to be convincing—to seem like real life. In real life, few things that happen come complete with explanations. We have to puzzle out the explanations for ourselves.

Stories, too, ask us to work out many explanations for ourselves. And the answers to our questions are in the story, waiting to be found. Every good author puts into a story all that a reader must know to understand what is happening and why. As we figure out for ourselves why the things an author puts in a story are there, we are interpreting what we read. To interpret a story is to explain its meaning—what happens in it, and why, and what the story is about.

## ACTIVE READING

You will need to think hard about the stories you read in Junior Great Books—not just about *what* happens but also about *why* it happens the way it does. You will be reading each story at least twice. When you read a story for the first time, your mind is mainly on the action—on what the characters think, do, and say. As you read, the main question you ask is likely to be "What's going to happen next?" When you read a story for the second time, your mind will be free to raise new and different questions about it, and this will lead you to think of new questions to explore with your group. You will almost always notice details that you missed on your first reading, ones that can make you change your mind about why the characters behave as they do or how you feel about them. A second reading gives you the chance to think about the story as a whole without wondering what will happen next.

In shared inquiry, you will need to read with a pencil in hand and to make notes as you read. While you are reading, mark the words and passages in the story that strike you as really important, interesting, or surprising. Mark places that make you think of a question. Mark parts that give you ideas about what the story means. Your teacher or leader may also ask you to watch for particular things during your reading and to give them special attention. Your notes will remind you of your thoughts while reading and help you to find evidence to back up what you say.

## QUESTIONS OF FACT, INTERPRETATION, AND EVALUATION

There are three kinds of questions that can be asked about a story in Junior Great Books: questions of fact, questions of interpretation, and questions of evaluation.

**Questions of fact** ask you to recall particular details or events from a story. Everything the author puts into the story is a fact in that story, even if some of the things couldn't happen in real life. In "Through the Tunnel," the first story in this book, many of the facts are very close to what we see in our daily lives, but in other stories they won't be. A question of fact has only one correct answer.

Knowing and remembering the facts in a story is important. They are the basis for your opinions about the story's meaning. And you will use them to support your opinions.

Many times a leader will ask a factual question in order to get you to back up what you have said with evidence from the story. Suppose someone says, "Jerry thinks he is old enough to go swimming by himself." A leader might then ask, *How old is Jerry?* This question can be answered by pointing to the place in the story that reads "He was an only child, eleven years old."

Now and then you will be asked a factual question that cannot be answered by looking at any one passage. For example, the question *Does Jerry's mother want him to be happy?* can only be answered "Yes." Although the story does not come right out and say so, her behavior shows that she does. Nothing in the story shows that she does not want him to be happy.

**Questions of interpretation** hold the central place in Junior Great Books. These are the questions that ask you to think carefully about what happens in a story and to consider what the story means. Unlike factual questions, they have more than a single good answer. Any answer that can be supported by factual evidence from the story will be a good one.

Some interpretive questions focus on a single passage or ask about a single event. Take, for example, this one: *Why does Jerry want to be with the other boys?* One answer is that he looks up to them because they are older. Another, that he feels lonely. Still another is that he recognizes that the boys are at home on this coast, and can let him in on its secrets.

Other, more basic interpretive questions are asked about the meaning of the story as a whole. The answers will often be drawn from several places in the story. Here is one basic interpretive question for "Through the Tunnel": *Why does Jerry keep the tunnel a secret from his mother?* No one passage answers this question, but the author gives a number of clues about Jerry's character: he wants badly to strike off on his own, he is worried about hurting his mother's feelings, and he finds the idea of swimming through the tunnel frightening. Remembering each of these things will help you decide how to begin answering this question.

**Questions of evaluation** ask how the story fits with your own experience and, after you have interpreted it, whether or not you agree with what the story is saying. As you read "Through the Tunnel," you might wonder, *Is it foolish to risk your life unnecessarily?* or *Wasn't it wrong for Jerry to keep his plan a secret from his mother?* In answering questions like these, you will be thinking more about yourself and your beliefs than about the story itself. After reading the story, thinking about evaluative questions can be a good way of deciding how you feel about the author's ideas.

Since understanding literature is the main purpose of Junior Great Books, you will spend most of your time considering questions of interpretation. Questions of fact will help you support your opinions about what a story means. Questions of evaluation will help you put yourself in the place of the characters in the story. You will have many chances to answer evaluative questions in your writing after Shared Inquiry Discussion.

## SHARED INQUIRY DISCUSSION

After you have read a story twice, taken notes, and shared some of your questions with your classmates, you will be ready to participate in Shared Inquiry Discussion. Shared Inquiry Discussion begins when the discussion leader asks an interpretive question, a question that can have more than one good answer. The leader is not sure which answer is the best, and hopes to discover several good answers during the discussion. Because there can be more than one good answer, it takes many minds to discover and explore those answers fully. By asking questions, the leader seeks to help everyone in the group think for themselves about what the story means.

# THE RULES OF SHARED INQUIRY DISCUSSION

1. **Only people who have read the story may take part in Shared Inquiry Discussion.** If you haven't read the story, you can't help others understand its meaning. Ideas that do not come from firsthand knowledge of the story will confuse the other members of the group.

2. **Discuss only the story everyone has read.** If you try to use other stories or personal experiences to explain your ideas, those who aren't familiar with them won't be able to join in the discussion.

3. **Do not use other people's opinions about the story unless you can back them up with evidence of your own.** When you take another person's word for what the story means, you have stopped thinking for yourself. This rule does not mean you may never use an idea you get from someone else. But make sure you understand the idea and can support it with factual details from the story.

4. **Leaders may only ask questions; they may not answer them.** Leaders never offer their own opinions. Instead, they share their questions about the story's meaning. This rule encourages you to do your own thinking about the story, and to remember that the leader really wants your help in understanding it.

In Shared Inquiry Discussion you may speak directly to anyone in the group, and not just to the leader. You may ask questions of anyone but the leader, and you will be answering questions that others ask you. Since you are all working together to search for a story's meaning, try to listen carefully when others are speaking. If you don't understand what they are saying, ask them to repeat their comments or explain them more clearly. If you disagree with what they are saying, you can tell them so, always giving your reasons. Sometimes, too, you will be able to support what another member of the group has said by giving a reason no one else has thought of.

By the end of a good discussion everyone in your group will understand the story better than they did before you began to exchange ideas, build on one another's insights, and work out new interpretations. At the close of a discussion, everyone will seldom agree in every detail on what the story means, but that's part of what makes it interesting and fun to discuss the stories in Junior Great Books.

# WRITING YOUR OWN
# INTERPRETIVE QUESTIONS

Writing interpretive questions is one of the best ways to think on your own about the meaning of a story. After you have read a story twice and taken notes, you will be ready to begin turning your ideas into interpretive questions. Some of the good ways to find interpretive questions are listed here, together with questions that were written for "Through the Tunnel."

**Look for words or passages that you think are important and that you wonder about.** One reader was puzzled by a word in this sentence: "And he almost ran after her again, feeling it unbearable that she should go by herself, but he did not." The reader wrote this interpretive question:

> *When Jerry first goes to the rocks, why does he feel it "unbearable" that his mother should go to the beach by herself?*

**Look for parts of the story that you feel strongly about.** As you read a story, ask questions about whatever makes you react with strong feelings. Look for places where you agree or disagree with the characters or with the author. For instance, one reader couldn't believe it when Jerry shouted and waggled his ears at the older boys, knowing that it would make him look and feel foolish. She asked:

> *Why does Jerry keep trying to get the boys' attention in a way that makes him feel ashamed?*

**When you are curious about why a character in the story acts the way he or she does, ask a question about that.** One reader, for example, was curious about Jerry's feelings when he swims out past the promontory to look for his mother on her beach. He wrote this question:

> *Why does being sure that his mother is there make Jerry feel both relieved and lonely?*

**Let questions come out of your ideas about the meaning of the story.** As you read, keep asking yourself what the author wants you to think about and experience through his or her words. Ask questions about that. One reader wondered why "Through the Tunnel" focuses on Jerry's decision to do something so difficult and frightening. She asked:

> *Why does Jerry decide he must swim through the tunnel?*

Interpretation begins with questions, the questions that come to you as you read. In working out the answers, you will arrive at a clearer idea of how the parts of the story fit together and have a better idea of its meaning.

# THROUGH THE TUNNEL

*Doris Lessing*

Going to the shore on the first morning of the vacation, the young English boy stopped at a turning of the path and looked down at a wild and rocky bay, and then over to the crowded beach he knew so well from other years. His mother walked on in front of him, carrying a bright striped bag in one hand. Her other arm, swinging loose, was very white in the sun. The boy watched that white naked arm, and turned his eyes, which had a frown behind them, towards the bay and back again to his mother. When she felt he was not with her, she swung around. "Oh, there you are, Jerry!" she said. She looked impatient, then smiled. "Why, darling, would you rather not come with me? Would you rather—" She frowned, conscientiously worrying over what amusements he might secretly be longing for, which she had been too busy or too careless to imagine. He was very familiar with that anxious, apologetic smile. Contrition sent him running after her. And yet, as he ran, he looked back over his shoulder at the wild bay; and all morning, as he played on the safe beach, he was thinking of it.

Next morning, when it was time for the routine of swimming and sunbathing, his mother said, "Are you tired of the usual beach, Jerry? Would you like to go somewhere else?"

"Oh, no!" he said quickly, smiling at her out of that unfailing impulse of contrition—a sort of chivalry. Yet, walking down the path with her, he blurted out, "I'd like to go and have a look at those rocks down there."

She gave the idea her attention. It was a wild-looking place, and there was no one there; but she said, "Of course, Jerry. When you've had enough, come to the big beach. Or just go straight back to the villa, if you like." She walked away, that bare arm, now slightly reddened from yesterday's sun, swinging. And he almost ran after her again, feeling it unbearable that she should go by herself, but he did not.

She was thinking, Of course he's old enough to be safe without me. Have I been keeping him too close? He mustn't feel he ought to be with me. I must be careful.

He was an only child, eleven years old. She was a widow. She was determined to be neither possessive nor lacking in devotion. She went worrying off to her beach.

As for Jerry, once he saw that his mother had gained her beach, he began the steep descent to the bay. From where he was, high up among red-brown rocks, it was a scoop of moving blueish green fringed with white. As he went lower, he saw that it spread among small promontories and inlets

2

of rough, sharp rock, and the crisping, lapping surface showed stains of purple and darker blue. Finally, as he ran sliding and scraping down the last few yards, he saw an edge of white surf and the shallow, luminous movement of water over white sand, and, beyond that, a solid, heavy blue.

He ran straight into the water and began swimming. He was a good swimmer. He went out fast over the gleaming sand, over a middle region where rocks lay like discoloured monsters under the surface, and then he was in the real sea—a warm sea where irregular cold currents from the deep water shocked his limbs.

When he was so far out that he could look back not only on the little bay but past the promontory that was between it and the big beach, he floated on the buoyant surface and looked for his mother. There she was, a speck of yellow under an umbrella that looked like a slice of orange peel. He swam back to shore, relieved at being sure she was there, but all at once very lonely.

On the edge of a small cape that marked the side of the bay away from the promontory was a loose scatter of rocks. Above them, some boys were stripping off their clothes. They came running, naked, down to the rocks. The English boy swam towards them, but kept his distance at a stone's throw. They were of that coast; all of them were burned smooth dark brown and speaking a language he did not understand. To be with them, of them, was a craving that filled his whole body. He swam a little closer; they turned and watched him with narrowed, alert dark eyes. Then one smiled and waved. It was enough. In a minute, he had swum in and was on the rocks beside them, smiling with a desperate, nervous supplication. They shouted cheerful greetings at him; and then, as he preserved his nervous, uncomprehending smile, they understood that he was a foreigner strayed from his own beach, and they proceeded to forget him. But he was happy. He was with them.

They began diving again and again from a high point into a well of blue sea between rough, pointed rocks. After they had dived and come up, they swam around, hauled themselves up, and waited their turn to dive again. They were big boys—men, to Jerry. He dived, and they watched him; and when he swam around to take his place, they made way for him. He felt he was accepted and he dived again, carefully, proud of himself.

Soon the biggest of the boys poised himself, shot down into the water, and did not come up. The others stood about, watching. Jerry, after waiting for the sleek brown head to appear, let out a yell of warning; they looked at him idly and turned their eyes back towards the water. After a long time, the boy came up on the other side of a big dark rock, letting the air out of his lungs in a sputtering gasp and a shout of triumph. Immediately the rest of them dived in. One moment, the morning seemed full of chattering boys; the next, the air and the surface of the water were empty. But through the heavy blue, dark shapes could be seen moving and groping.

Jerry dived, shot past the school of underwater swimmers, saw a black wall of rock looming at him, touched it, and bobbed up at once to the surface, where the wall was a low barrier he could see across. There was no one visible; under him, in the water, the dim shapes of the swimmers had disappeared. Then one, and then another of the boys came up on the far side of the barrier of rock, and he understood that they had swum through some gap or hole in it. He plunged down again. He could see nothing through the stinging salt water but the blank rock. When he came up the boys were all on the diving rock, preparing to attempt the feat again. And now, in a panic of failure, he yelled up, in English, "Look at me! Look!" and he began splashing and kicking in the water like a foolish dog.

They looked down gravely, frowning. He knew the frown. At moments of failure, when he clowned to claim his mother's attention, it was with just this grave, embarrassed inspection that she rewarded him. Through his hot shame, feeling the pleading grin on his face like a scar that he could never remove, he looked up at the group of big brown boys on the rock and shouted *"Bonjour! Merci! Au revoir! Monsieur, monsieur!"* while he hooked his fingers round his ears and waggled them.

Water surged into his mouth; he choked, sank, came up. The rock, lately weighted with boys, seemed to rear up out of the water as their weight was removed. They were flying down past him now, into the water; the air was full of falling bodies. Then the rock was empty in the hot sunlight. He counted one, two, three . . .

At fifty, he was terrified. They must all be drowning beneath him, in the watery caves of the rock! At a hundred, he stared around him at the empty hillside, wondering if he should yell for help. He counted faster, faster, to hurry them up, to bring them to the surface quickly, to drown them quickly—anything rather than the terror of counting on and on into the blue emptiness of the morning. And then, at a hundred and sixty, the water beyond the rock was full of boys blowing like brown whales. They swam back to the shore without a look at him.

He climbed back to the diving rock and sat down, feeling the hot roughness of it under his thighs. The boys were gathering up their bits of clothing and running off along the shore to another promontory. They were leaving to get away from him. He cried openly, fists in his eyes. There was no one to see him, and he cried himself out.

It seemed to him that a long time had passed, and he swam out to where he could see his mother. Yes, she was still there, a yellow spot under an orange umbrella. He swam back to the big rock, climbed up, and dived into the blue pool among the fanged and angry boulders. Down he went, until he touched the wall of rock again. But the salt was so painful in his eyes that he could not see.

He came to the surface, swam to shore, and went back to the villa to wait for his mother. Soon she walked slowly up the path, swinging her striped bag, the flushed, naked arm dangling beside her. "I want some swimming goggles," he panted, defiant and beseeching.

She gave him a patient, inquisitive look as she said casually, "Well, of course, darling."

But now, now, now! He must have them this minute, and no other time. He nagged and pestered until she went with him to a shop. As soon as she had bought the goggles, he grabbed them from her hand as if she were going to claim them for herself, and was off, running down the steep path to the bay.

Jerry swam out to the big barrier rock, adjusted the goggles, and dived. The impact of the water broke the rubber-enclosed vacuum, and the goggles came loose. He understood that he must swim down to the base of the rock from the surface of the water. He fixed the goggles tight and firm, filled his lungs, and floated, face down, on the water. Now he could see. It was as if he had eyes of a different kind—fish eyes that showed everything clear and delicate and wavering in the bright water.

Under him, six or seven feet down, was a floor of perfectly clean, shining white sand, rippled firm and hard by the tides. Two greyish shapes steered there, like long, rounded pieces of wood or slate. They were fish. He saw them nose towards each other, poise motionless, make a dart forward, swerve off, and come around again. It was like a water dance. A few inches above them the water sparkled as if sequins were dropping through it. Fish again—myriads of minute fish, the length of his fingernail—were drifting through the water, and in a moment he could feel the innumerable tiny touches of them against his limbs. It was like swimming in flaked silver. The great rock the big boys had swum through rose sheer out of the white sand—black, tufted lightly with greenish weed. He could see no gap in it. He swam down to its base.

Again and again he rose, took a big chestful of air, and went down. Again and again he groped over the surface of the rock, feeling it, almost hugging it in the desperate need

to find the entrance. And then, once, while he was clinging
to the black wall, his knees came up and he shot his feet
out forward and they met no obstacle. He had found
the hole.

He gained the surface, clambered about the stones that
littered the barrier rock until he found a big one, and, with
this in his arms, let himself down over the side of the rock.
He dropped, with the weight, straight to the sandy floor.
Clinging tight to the anchor of stone, he lay on his side
and looked in under the dark shelf at the place where his
feet had gone. He could see the hole. It was an irregular,
dark gap; but he could not see deep into it. He let go of
his anchor, clung with his hands to the edges of the hole,
and tried to push himself in.

He got his head in, found his shoulders jammed,
moved them in sidewise, and was inside as far as his
waist. He could see nothing ahead. Something soft and
clammy touched his mouth; he saw a dark frond moving
against the greyish rock, and panic filled him. He thought
of octopuses, of clinging weed. He pushed himself out
backward and caught a glimpse, as he retreated, of a
harmless tentacle of seaweed drifting in the mouth of the
tunnel. But it was enough. He reached the sunlight, swam
to shore, and lay on the diving rock. He looked down
into the blue well of water. He knew he must find his
way through that cave, or hole, or tunnel, and out the
other side.

First, he thought, he must learn to control his breathing.
He let himself down into the water with another big stone
in his arms, so that he could lie effortlessly on the bottom

of the sea. He counted. One, two, three. He counted steadily. He could hear the movement of blood in his chest. Fifty-one, fifty-two . . . His chest was hurting. He let go of the rock and went up into the air. He saw that the sun was low. He rushed to the villa and found his mother at her supper. She said only, "Did you enjoy yourself?" and he said, "Yes."

All night the boy dreamed of the water-filled cave in the rock, and as soon as breakfast was over he went to the bay.

That night, his nose bled badly. For hours he had been underwater, learning to hold his breath, and now he felt weak and dizzy. His mother said, "I shouldn't overdo things, darling, if I were you."

That day and the next, Jerry exercised his lungs as if everything, the whole of his life, all that he would become, depended upon it. Again his nose bled at night, and his mother insisted on his coming with her the next day. It was a torment to him to waste a day of his careful self-training, but he stayed with her on that other beach, which now seemed a place for small children, a place where his mother might lie safe in the sun. It was not his beach.

He did not ask for permission, on the following day, to go to his beach. He went, before his mother could consider the complicated rights and wrongs of the matter. A day's rest, he discovered, had improved his count by ten. The big boys had made the passage while he counted a hundred and sixty. He had been counting fast, in his fright. Probably now, if he tried, he could get through that long tunnel, but he was not going to try yet. A curious, most unchildlike persistence, a controlled impatience, made him wait. In the meantime, he lay underwater on the white sand, littered now by stones he had brought down from the upper air, and studied the entrance to the tunnel. He knew every jut and corner of it, as far as it was possible to see. It was as if he already felt its sharpness about his shoulders.

He sat by the clock in the villa, when his mother was not near, and checked his time. He was incredulous and then proud to find he could hold his breath without strain for two minutes. The words "two minutes," authorised by the clock, brought close the adventure that was so necessary to him.

In another four days, his mother said casually one morning, they must go home. On the day before they left, he would do it. He would do it if it killed him, he said defiantly to himself. But two days before they were to leave—a day of triumph when he increased his count by fifteen—his nose bled so badly that he turned dizzy and had to lie limply over the big rock like a bit of seaweed, watching the thick red blood flow onto the rock and trickle slowly down to the sea. He was frightened. Supposing he turned dizzy in the tunnel? Supposing he died there, trapped? Supposing—his head went around, in the hot sun, and he almost gave up. He thought he would return to the house and lie down, and next summer, perhaps, when he had another year's growth in him—*then* he would go through the hole.

But even after he had made the decision, or thought he had, he found himself sitting up on the rock and looking down into the water; and he knew that now, this moment, when his nose had only just stopped bleeding, when his head was still sore and throbbing—this was the moment when he would try. If he did not do it now, he never would. He was trembling with fear that he would not go; and he was trembling with horror at the long, long tunnel under the rock, under the sea. Even in the open sunlight, the barrier rock seemed very wide and very heavy; tons of rock pressed down on where he would go. If he died there, he would lie until one day—perhaps not before next year— those big boys would swim into it and find it blocked.

He put on his goggles, fitted them tight, tested the vacuum. His hands were shaking. Then he chose the biggest stone he could carry and slipped over the edge of the rock until half of him was in the cool enclosing water and half in the hot sun. He looked up once at the empty sky, filled his lungs once, twice, and then sank fast to the bottom with the stone. He let it go and began to count. He took the edges of the hole in his hands and drew himself into it, wriggling his shoulders in sidewise as he remembered he must, kicking himself along with his feet.

Soon he was clear inside. He was in a small rock-bound hole filled with yellowish-grey water. The water was pushing him up against the roof. The roof was sharp and pained his back. He pulled himself along with his hands— fast, fast—and used his legs as levers. His head knocked against something; a sharp pain dizzied him. Fifty, fifty-one, fifty-two . . . He was without light, and the water seemed to press upon him with the weight of rock. Seventy-one, seventy-two . . . There was no strain on his lungs. He felt like an inflated balloon, his lungs were so light and easy, but his head was pulsing.

He was being continually pressed against the sharp roof, which felt slimy as well as sharp. Again he thought of octopuses, and wondered if the tunnel might be filled with weed that could tangle him. He gave himself a panicky, convulsive kick forward, ducked his head, and swam. His feet and hands moved freely, as if in open water. The hole must have widened out. He thought he must be swimming fast, and he was frightened of banging his head if the tunnel narrowed.

A hundred, a hundred and one . . . The water paled. Victory filled him. His lungs were beginning to hurt. A few more strokes and he would be out. He was counting wildly; he said a hundred and fifteen, and then, a long time later, a hundred and fifteen again. The water was a clear jewel-green all around him. Then he saw, above his head, a crack running up through the rock. Sunlight was falling through it, showing the clean, dark rock of the tunnel, a single mussel shell, and darkness ahead.

He was at the end of what he could do. He looked up at the crack as if it were filled with air and not water, as if he could put his mouth to it to draw in air. A hundred and fifteen, he heard himself say inside his head—but he had said that long ago. He must go on into the blackness ahead, or he would drown. His head was swelling, his lungs cracking. A hundred and fifteen, a hundred and fifteen pounded through his head, and he feebly clutched at rocks in the dark, pulling himself forward, leaving the brief space of sunlit water behind. He felt he was dying. He was no longer quite conscious. He struggled on in the darkness between lapses into unconsciousness. An immense, swelling pain filled his head, and then the darkness cracked with an explosion of green light. His hands, groping forward, met nothing; and his feet, kicking back, propelled him out into the open sea.

He drifted to the surface, his face turned up to the air. He was gasping like a fish. He felt he would sink now and drown; he could not swim the few feet back to the rock. Then he was clutching it and pulling himself up onto it. He lay face down, gasping. He could see nothing but a red-veined, clotted dark. His eyes must have burst, he thought; they were full of blood. He tore off his goggles and a gout of blood went into the sea. His nose was bleeding, and the blood had filled the goggles.

He scooped up handfuls of water from the cool, salty sea, to splash on his face, and did not know whether it was blood or salt water he tasted. After a time, his heart quieted, his eyes cleared, and he sat up. He could see the local boys diving and playing half a mile away. He did not want them. He wanted nothing but to get back home and lie down.

In a short while, Jerry swam to shore and climbed slowly up the path to the villa. He flung himself on his bed and slept, waking at the sound of feet on the path outside. His mother was coming back. He rushed to the bathroom, thinking she must not see his face with bloodstains, or tearstains, on it. He came out of the bathroom and met her as she walked into the villa, smiling, her eyes lighting up.

"Have a nice morning?" she asked, laying her hand on his warm brown shoulder a moment.

"Oh, yes, thank you," he said.

"You look a bit pale." And then, sharp and anxious, "How did you bang your head?"

"Oh, just banged it," he told her.

She looked at him closely. He was strained; his eyes were glazed-looking. She was worried. And then she said to herself, Oh, don't fuss! Nothing can happen. He can swim like a fish.

They sat down to lunch together.

"Mummy," he said, "I can stay underwater for two minutes—three minutes, at least." It came bursting out of him.

"Can you, darling?" she said. "Well, I shouldn't overdo it. I don't think you ought to swim anymore today."

She was ready for a battle of wills, but he gave in at once. It was no longer of the least importance to go to the bay.

# RAYMOND'S RUN

*Toni Cade Bambara*

I don't have much work to do around the house like some girls. My mother does that. And I don't have to earn my pocket money by hustling; George runs errands for the big boys and sells Christmas cards. And anything else that's got to get done, my father does. All I have to do in life is mind my brother Raymond, which is enough.

Sometimes I slip and say my little brother Raymond. But as any fool can see he's much bigger and he's older too. But a lot of people call him my little brother cause he needs looking after cause he's not quite right. And a lot of smart mouths got lots to say about that too, especially when George was minding him. But now, if anybody has anything to say to Raymond, anything to say about his big head, they have to come by me. And I don't play the dozens or believe in standing around with somebody in my face doing a lot of talking. I much rather just knock you down and take my chances even if I am a little girl with skinny arms and a squeaky voice, which is how I got the name Squeaky. And if things get too rough, I run. And as anybody can tell you, I'm the fastest thing on two feet.

There is no track meet that I don't win the first-place medal. I used to win the twenty-yard dash when I was a little kid in kindergarten. Nowadays, it's the fifty-yard dash. And tomorrow I'm subject to run the quarter-meter relay all by myself and come in first, second, and third. The big kids call me Mercury cause I'm the swiftest thing in the neighborhood. Everybody knows that—except two people who know better, my father and me. He can beat me to Amsterdam Avenue with me having a two-fire-hydrant headstart and him running with his hands in his pockets and whistling. But that's private information. Cause can you imagine some thirty-five-year-old man stuffing himself into PAL shorts to race little kids? So as far as everyone's concerned, I'm the fastest and that goes for Gretchen, too, who has put out the tale that she is going to win the first-place medal this year. Ridiculous. In the second place, she's got short legs. In the third place, she's got freckles. In the first place, no one can beat me and that's all there is to it.

I'm standing on the corner admiring the weather and about to take a stroll down Broadway so I can practice my breathing exercises, and I've got Raymond walking on the inside close to the buildings, cause he's subject to fits of fantasy and starts thinking he's a circus performer and that the curb is a tightrope strung high in the air. And sometimes after a rain he likes to step down off his tightrope right into the gutter and slosh around getting his shoes and cuffs wet. Then I get hit when I get home. Or sometimes if you don't watch him he'll dash across traffic to the island in the middle of Broadway and give the pigeons a fit. Then I have to go behind him apologizing to all the old people sitting around trying to get some sun and getting all upset with the pigeons fluttering around them, scattering their newspapers and upsetting the waxpaper lunches in their laps. So I keep Raymond on the inside of me, and he plays like he's driving a stagecoach which is OK by me so long as he doesn't run me over or interrupt my breathing exercises, which I have to do on account of I'm serious about my running, and I don't care who knows it.

Now some people like to act like things come easy to them, won't let on that they practice. Not me. I'll high-prance down 34th Street like a rodeo pony to keep my knees strong even if it does get my mother uptight so that she walks ahead like she's not with me, don't know me, is all by herself on a shopping trip, and I am somebody else's crazy child. Now you take Cynthia Procter for instance. She's just the opposite. If there's a test tomorrow, she'll say something like, "Oh, I guess I'll play handball this afternoon and watch television tonight," just to let you know she ain't thinking about the test. Or like last week when she won the spelling bee for the millionth time, "A good thing you got 'receive,' Squeaky, cause I would have got it wrong. I completely forgot about the spelling bee." And she'll clutch the lace on her blouse like it was a narrow escape. Oh, brother. But of course when I pass her house on my early morning trots around the block, she is practicing the scales on the piano over and over and over and over. Then in music class she always lets herself get bumped around so she falls accidently on purpose onto the piano stool and is so surprised to find herself sitting there that she decides just for fun to try out the ole keys. And what do you know—Chopin's waltzes just spring out of her fingertips and she's the most surprised thing in the world. A regular prodigy. I could kill people like that. I stay up all night studying the words for the spelling bee. And you can see me any time of day practicing running. I never walk if I can trot, and shame on Raymond if he can't keep up. But of course he does, cause if he hangs back someone's liable to walk up to him and get smart, or take his allowance from him, or ask him where he got that great big pumpkin head. People are so stupid sometimes.

So I'm strolling down Broadway breathing out and breathing in on counts of seven, which is my lucky number, and here comes Gretchen and her sidekicks: Mary Louise, who used to be a friend of mine when she first moved to Harlem from Baltimore and got beat up by everybody till I took up for her on account of her mother and my mother used to sing in the same choir when they were young girls, but people ain't grateful, so now she hangs out with the new girl Gretchen and talks about me like a dog; and Rosie, who is as fat as I am skinny and has a big mouth where Raymond is concerned and is too stupid to know that there is not a big deal of difference between herself and Raymond and that she can't afford to throw stones. So they are steady coming up Broadway and I see right away that it's going to be one of those Dodge City scenes cause the street ain't that big and they're close to the buildings just as we are. First I think I'll step into the candy store and look over the new comics and let them pass. But that's chicken and I've got a reputation to consider. So then I think I'll just walk straight on through them or even over them if necessary. But as they get to me, they slow down. I'm ready to fight, cause like I said I don't feature a whole lot of chit-chat, I much prefer to just knock you down right from the jump and save everybody a lotta precious time.

"You signing up for the May Day races?" smiles Mary Louise, only it's not a smile at all. A dumb question like that doesn't deserve an answer. Besides, there's just me and Gretchen standing there really, so no use wasting my breath talking to shadows.

"I don't think you're going to win this time," says Rosie, trying to signify with her hands on her hips all salty, completely forgetting that I have whupped her behind many times for less salt than that.

"I always win cause I'm the best," I say straight at Gretchen who is, as far as I'm concerned, the only one talking in this ventriloquist-dummy routine. Gretchen smiles, but it's not a smile, and I'm thinking that girls never really smile at each other because they don't know how and don't want to know how and there's probably no one to teach us how, cause grown-up girls don't know either. Then they all look at Raymond who has just brought his mule team to a standstill. And they're about to see what trouble they can get into through him.

"What grade you in now, Raymond?"

"You got anything to say to my brother, you say it to me, Mary Louise Williams of Raggedy Town, Baltimore."

"What are you, his mother?" sasses Rosie.

"That's right, Fatso. And the next word out of anybody and I'll be *their* mother too." So they just stand there and Gretchen shifts from one leg to the other and so do they. Then Gretchen puts her hands on her hips and is about to say something with her freckle-face self but doesn't. Then she walks around me looking me up and down but keeps walking up Broadway, and her sidekicks follow her. So me and Raymond smile at each other and he says, "Gidyap" to his team and I continue with my breathing exercises, strolling down Broadway toward the ice man on 145th with not a care in the world cause I am Miss Quicksilver herself.

I take my time getting to the park on May Day because the track meet is the last thing on the program. The biggest thing on the program is the May Pole dancing, which I can do without, thank you, even if my mother thinks it's a shame I don't take part and act like a girl for a change. You'd think my mother'd be grateful not to have to make me a white organdy dress with a big satin sash and buy me new white baby-doll shoes that can't be taken out of the box till the big day. You'd think she'd be glad her daughter ain't out there prancing around a May Pole getting the new clothes all dirty and sweaty and trying to act like a fairy or a flower or whatever you're supposed to be when you should be trying to be yourself, whatever that is, which is, as far as I am concerned, a poor Black girl who really can't afford to buy shoes and a new dress you only wear once a lifetime cause it won't fit next year.

I was once a strawberry in a Hansel and Gretel pageant when I was in nursery school and didn't have no better sense than to dance on tiptoe with my arms in a circle over my head doing umbrella steps and being a perfect fool just so my mother and father could come dressed up and clap. You'd think they'd know better than to encourage that kind of nonsense. I am not a strawberry. I do not dance on my toes. I run. That is what I am all about. So I always come late to the May Day program, just in time to get my number pinned on and lay in the grass till they announce the fifty-yard dash.

I put Raymond in the little swings, which is a tight squeeze this year and will be impossible next year. Then I look around for Mr. Pearson, who pins the numbers on. I'm really looking for Gretchen if you want to know the truth, but she's not around. The park is jam-packed. Parents in hats and corsages and breast-pocket handkerchiefs peeking up. Kids in white dresses and light-blue suits. The parkees unfolding chairs and chasing the rowdy kids from Lenox as if they had no right to be there. The big guys with their caps on backwards, leaning against the fence swirling the basketballs on the tips of their fingers, waiting for all these crazy people to clear out the park so they can play. Most of the kids in my class are carrying bass drums and glockenspiels and flutes. You'd think they'd put in a few bongos or something for real like that.

Then here comes Mr. Pearson with his clipboard and his cards and pencils and whistles and safety pins and fifty million other things he's always dropping all over the place with his clumsy self. He sticks out in a crowd because he's on stilts. We used to call him Jack and the Beanstalk to get him mad. But I'm the only one that can outrun him and get away, and I'm too grown for that silliness now.

"Well, Squeaky," he says, checking my name off the list and handing me number seven and two pins. And I'm thinking he's got no right to call me Squeaky, if I can't call him Beanstalk.

"Hazel Elizabeth Deborah Parker," I correct him and tell him to write it down on his board.

"Well, Hazel Elizabeth Deborah Parker, going to give someone else a break this year?" I squint at him real hard to see if he is seriously thinking I should lose the race on purpose just to give someone else a break. "Only six girls running this time," he continues, shaking his head sadly like it's my fault all of New York didn't turn out in sneakers. "That new girl should give you a run for your money." He looks around the park for Gretchen like a periscope in a submarine movie. "Wouldn't it be a nice gesture if you were . . . to ahhh . . ."

I give him such a look he couldn't finish putting that idea into words. Grownups got a lot of nerve sometimes. I pin number seven to myself and stomp away, I'm so burnt. And I go straight for the track and stretch out on the grass while the band winds up with "Oh, the Monkey Wrapped His Tail Around the Flag Pole," which my teacher calls by some other name. The man on the loudspeaker is calling everyone over to the track and I'm on my back looking at the sky, trying to pretend I'm in the country, but I can't, because even grass in the city feels hard as sidewalk, and there's just no pretending you are anywhere but in a "concrete jungle" as my grandfather says.

22

The twenty-yard dash takes all of two minutes cause most of the little kids don't know no better than to run off the track or run the wrong way or run smack into the fence and fall down and cry. One little kid, though, has got the good sense to run straight for the white ribbon up ahead so he wins. Then the second-graders line up for the thirty-yard dash and I don't even bother to turn my head to watch cause Raphael Perez always wins. He wins before he even begins by psyching the runners, telling them they're going to trip on their shoelaces and fall on their faces or lose their shorts or something, which he doesn't really have to do since he is very fast, almost as fast as I am. After that is the forty-yard dash which I use to run when I was in first grade. Raymond is hollering from the swings cause he knows I'm about to do my thing cause the man on the loudspeaker has just announced the fifty-yard dash, although he might just as well be giving a recipe for angel food cake cause you can hardly make out what he's sayin for the static. I get up and slip off my sweat pants and then I see Gretchen standing at the starting line, kicking her legs out like a pro. Then as I get into place I see that ole Raymond is on line on the other side of the fence, bending down with his fingers on the ground just like he knew what he was doing. I was going to yell at him but then I didn't. It burns up your energy to holler.

Every time, just before I take off in a race, I always feel like I'm in a dream, the kind of dream you have when you're sick with fever and feel all hot and weightless. I dream I'm flying over a sandy beach in the early morning sun, kissing the leaves of the trees as I fly by. And there's

23

always the smell of apples, just like in the country when I was little and used to think I was a choo-choo train, running through the fields of corn and chugging up the hill to the orchard. And all the time I'm dreaming this, I get lighter and lighter until I'm flying over the beach again, getting blown through the sky like a feather that weighs nothing at all. But once I spread my fingers in the dirt and crouch over the Get on Your Mark, the dream goes and I am solid again and am telling myself, Squeaky you must win, you must win, you are the fastest thing in the world, you can even beat your father up Amsterdam if you really try. And then I feel my weight coming back just behind my knees then down to my feet then into the earth and the pistol shot explodes in my blood and I am off and weightless again, flying past the other runners, my arms pumping up and down and the whole world is quiet except for the crunch as I zoom over the gravel in the track. I glance to my left and there is no one. To the right, a blurred Gretchen, who's got her chin jutting out as if it would win the race all by itself. And on the other side of the fence is Raymond with his arms down to his side and the palms tucked up behind him, running in his very own style, and it's the first time I ever saw that and I almost stop to watch my brother Raymond on his first run. But the white ribbon is bouncing toward me and I tear past it, racing into the distance till my feet with a mind of their own start digging up footfuls of dirt and brake me short. Then all the kids standing on the side pile on me, banging me on the back and slapping my head with their May Day programs, for I have won again and everybody on 151st Street can walk tall for another year.

"In first place . . ." the man on the loudspeaker is clear as a bell now. But then he pauses and the loudspeaker starts to whine. Then static. And I lean down to catch my breath and here comes Gretchen walking back, for she's overshot the finish line too, huffing and puffing with her hands on her hips taking it slow, breathing in steady time like a real pro and I sort of like her a little for the first time. "In first place . . ." and then three or four voices get all mixed up on the loudspeaker and I dig my sneaker into the grass and stare at Gretchen who's staring back, we both wondering just who did win. I can hear old Beanstalk arguing with the man on the loudspeaker and then a few others running their mouths about what the stopwatches say. Then I hear Raymond yanking at the fence to call me and I wave to shush him, but he keeps rattling the fence like a gorilla in a cage like in them gorilla movies, but then like a dancer or something he starts climbing up nice and easy but very fast. And it occurs to me, watching how smoothly he climbs hand over hand and remembering how he looked running with his arms down to his side and with the wind pulling his mouth back and his teeth showing and all, it occurred to me that Raymond would make a very fine runner. Doesn't he always keep up with me on my trots? And he surely knows how to breathe in counts of seven cause he's always doing it at the dinner table, which drives my brother George up the wall. And I'm smiling to beat the band cause if I've lost this race, or if me and Gretchen tied, or even if I've won, I can always retire as a runner and begin a whole new career as a coach with Raymond as my champion. After all, with a little more study I can beat Cynthia and her phony self at the spelling bee. And if I bugged my mother, I could get piano lessons and become a star. And I have a big rep as the baddest thing around. And I've got a roomful of ribbons and medals and awards. But what has Raymond got to call his own?

So I stand there with my new plans, laughing out loud by this time as Raymond jumps down from the fence and runs over with his teeth showing and his arms down to the side, which no one before him has quite mastered as a running style. And by the time he comes over I'm jumping up and down so glad to see him—my brother Raymond, a great runner in the family tradition. But of course everyone thinks I'm jumping up and down because the men on the loudspeaker have finally gotten themselves together and compared notes and are announcing "In first place— Miss Hazel Elizabeth Deborah Parker." (Dig that.) "In second place—Miss Gretchen P. Lewis." And I look over at Gretchen wondering what the "P" stands for. And I smile. Cause she's good, no doubt about it. Maybe she'd like to help me coach Raymond; she obviously is serious about running, as any fool can see. And she nods to congratulate me and then she smiles. And I smile. We stand there with this big smile of respect between us. It's about as real a smile as girls can do for each other, considering we don't practice real smiling every day, you know, cause maybe we too busy being flowers or fairies or strawberries instead of something honest and worthy of respect . . . you know . . . like being people.

# MY GREATEST AMBITION

*Morris Lurie*

My greatest ambition was to be a comic-strip artist, but I grew out of it. People were always patting me on the head and saying, "He'll grow out of it." They didn't know what they were talking about. Had any of them ever read a comic? Studied one? *Drawn* one? "Australia is no place for comics," they said, and I had to lock myself up in the dining room to get some peace. My mother thought I was studying in there.

I was the only person in my class—probably in the whole school—who wanted to be a comic-strip artist. They were all dreamers. There they sat, the astronomer, the nuclear physicist, the business tycoon (on the Stock Exchange), two mathematicians, three farmers, countless chemists, a handful of doctors, all aged thirteen and all with their heads in the clouds. Dreamers! Idle speculators! A generation of hopeless romantics! It was a Friday night,

I recall, when I put the finishing touches to my first full-length, inked-in, original, six-page comic strip.

I didn't have the faintest idea what to do with it. Actually, doing anything *with* it hadn't ever entered my mind. *Doing* it was enough. Over the weekend I read it through sixty or seventy times, analysed it, studied it, stared at it, finally pronounced it "Not too bad," and then put it up on the top of my wardrobe where my father kept his hats.

And that would have been the end of it, only the next day I happened to mention to Michael Lazarus, who sat next to me at school, that I had drawn a comic strip, and he happened to mention to me that there was a magazine in Melbourne I could send it to. We were both thrown out of that class for doing too much mentioning out loud, and kept in after school, to write fifty eight-letter words and their meanings in sentences—a common disciplinary action at that time. I remember writing *ambulate* and saying it was a special way of walking. Do I digress? Then let me say the first thing I did when I got home was roll my comic up in brown paper, address it, and put it in my schoolbag where I wouldn't forget it in the morning. Some chance of that. Lazarus had introduced an entirely new idea into my head. Publication. I hardly slept all night.

One of the things that kept me tossing and turning was the magazine I was sending my comic to. *Boy Magazine.* I had never bought one in my life, because it had the sneaky policy of printing stories, with only one illustration at the top of the page to get you interested. *Stories?* The school library was full of them, and what a bore they were. Did I want my comic to appear in a magazine which printed stories, where it would be read by the sort of people who were always taking books out of the library and sitting under trees and wearing glasses and squinting and turning pages with licked fingers? An *awful* prospect! At two o'clock in the morning I decided no, I didn't, and at three I did, and at four it was no again, but the last thing I saw before I finally fell asleep was Lazarus's face and he was saying, "Publication!" and that decided it. Away it went.

Now let me properly introduce my father, a great scoffer. In those pre-television days, he had absolutely nothing to do in the evening but to walk past my room and look in and say, "Nu? They sent you the money yet?" Fifty times a night, at least. And when the letter came from *Boy Magazine,* did he change his tune? Not one bit.

"I don't see a cheque," he said.

"Of *course* there's no cheque," I said. "How can there be? We haven't even discussed it yet. Maybe I'll decide not to sell it to them. Which I will, if their price isn't right."

"Show me again the letter," my father said. "Ha, listen, listen. 'We are very interested in your comic and would like you to phone Miss Gordon to make an appointment to see the editor.' An appointment? That means they don't want it. If they wanted it, believe me, there'd be a cheque."

It serves no purpose to put down the rest of this pointless conversation, which included such lines as "How many comics have *you* sold in your life?" and, "Who paid for the paper? The ink?" other than to say that I made the phone call to Miss Gordon from a public phone and not from home. I wasn't going to have my father listening to every word.

29

My voice, when I was thirteen, and standing on tiptoe and talking into a public phone, was, I must admit, unnecessarily loud, but Miss Gordon didn't say anything about it. "And what day will be most convenient for you, Mr. Lurie?" she asked. "Oh, any day at all!" I shouted. "Any day will suit me fine!" "A week from Thursday then?" she asked. "Perfect!" I yelled, trying to get a piece of paper and a pencil out of my trouser pocket to write it down, and at the same time listening like mad in case Miss Gordon said something else. And she did. "Ten o'clock?" "I'll be there!" I shouted, and hung up with a crash.

It hadn't occurred to me to mention to Miss Gordon that I was thirteen and at school and would have to take a day off to come and see the editor. I didn't think these things were relevant to our business. But my mother did. A day missed from school could never be caught up, that was her attitude. My father's attitude you know. A cheque or not a cheque. Was I rich or was I a fool? (No, that's wrong. Was I a poor fool or a rich fool? Yes, that's better.) But my problem was something else. What to wear?

My school suit was out of the question because I wore it every day and I was sick of it and it just wasn't right for a business appointment. Anyway, it had ink stains round the pocket where my fountain pen leaked (a real fountain, ha ha), and the seat of the trousers shone like a piece of tin. And my Good Suit was a year old and too short in the leg. I tried it on in front of the mirror, just to make sure, and I was right. It was ludicrous. My father offered to lend me one of his suits. He hadn't bought a new suit since 1934. There was enough material in the lapels alone to make three suits and have enough left over for a couple of caps. Not only that, but my father was shorter than me and twice the weight. So I thanked him and said that I had decided to wear my Good Suit after all. I would wear dark socks and the shortness of trousers would hardly be noticed. Also, I would wear my eye-dazzling pure silk corn yellow tie, which, with the proper Windsor knot, would so ruthlessly rivet attention that no one would even look to see if I was wearing shoes.

"A prince," my father said.

Now, as the day of my appointment drew nearer and nearer, a great question had to be answered, a momentous decision made. For my father had been right. If all they wanted to do was to buy my comic, they would have sent a cheque. So there was something else. A full-time career as a comic-strip artist on the permanent staff of *Boy Magazine*! It had to be that. But that would mean giving up school and was I prepared to do that?

"Yes," I said with great calmness and great authority to my face in the bathroom mirror. "Yes."

There were three days to go.

Then there occurred one of those things that must happen every day in the world of big business, but when you're thirteen it knocks you for a loop. *Boy Magazine* sent me a telegram. It was the first telegram I had ever received in my life, and about the third that had ever come to our house. My mother opened it straight away. She told everyone in our street about it. She phoned uncles, aunts, sisters, brothers, and finally, when I came home from school, she told me.

I was furious. I shouted, "I told you never under *any* circumstances to open my mail!"

"But a telegram," my mother said.

"A telegram is mail," I said. "And mail is a personal, private thing. Where is it?"

My mother had folded it four times and put it in her purse and her purse in her bag and her bag in her wardrobe which she had locked. She stood by my side and watched me while I read it.

"Nu?" she said.

"It's nothing," I said.

And it wasn't. Miss Gordon had suddenly discovered that the editor was going to be out of town on my appointment day, and would I kindly phone and make another appointment?

I did, standing on tiptoe and shouting as before.

The offices of *Boy Magazine* were practically in the country, twelve train stations out of town. Trains, when I was thirteen, terrified me, and still do. Wearing my Good Suit and my corn yellow tie and my father's best black socks and a great scoop of oil in my hair, I kept jumping up from my seat and looking out of the window to see if we were getting near a station and then sitting down again and trying to relax. Twelve stations, eleven stations, ten. Nine to go, eight, seven. Or was it six? What was the name of the last one? What if I went too far? What was the time? By the time I arrived at the right station, I was in a fine state of nerves.

The offices of *Boy Magazine* were easy to find. They were part of an enormous building that looked like a factory, and were not at all imposing or impressive, as I had imagined them to be. No neon, no massive areas of plate glass, no exotic plants growing in white gravel. (I had a picture of myself walking to work every morning through a garden of exotic plants growing in white gravel, cacti, ferns, pushing open a massive glass door under a neon sign and smiling at a receptionist with a pipe in my mouth.) I pushed open an ordinary door and stepped into an ordinary foyer and told an ordinary lady sitting at an ordinary desk who I was.

"And?" she said.

"I have an appointment to see the editor of *Boy Magazine*," I said.

"Oh," she said.

"At ten o'clock," I said. "I think I'm early." It was half past nine.

"Just one minute," she said, and picked up a telephone. While she was talking I looked around the foyer, in which there was nothing to look at, but I don't like eavesdropping on people talking on the phone.

Then she put down the phone and said to me, "Won't be long. Would you like to take a seat?"

For some reason that caught me unawares and I flashed her a blinding smile and kept standing there, wondering what was going to happen next, and then I realized what she had said and I smiled again and turned around and bumped into a chair and sat down and crossed my legs and looked around and then remembered the shortness of my trousers and quickly uncrossed my legs and sat perfectly straight and still, except for looking at my watch ten times in the next thirty seconds.

I don't know how long I sat there. It was either five minutes or an hour, it's hard to say. The lady at the desk didn't seem to have anything to do, and I didn't like looking at her, but from time to time our eyes met, and I would smile—or was that smile stretched across my face from the second I came in? I used to do things like that when I was thirteen.

Finally a door opened and another lady appeared. She seemed, for some reason, quite surprised when she saw me sitting there, as though I had three eyes or was wearing a red suit, but I must say this for her, she had poise, she pulled herself together very quickly, hardly dropped a stitch, as it were, and holding open the door through which she had come, she said, "Won't you come this way?" and I did.

I was shown into an office that was filled with men in grey suits. Actually, there were only three of them, but they all stood up when I came in, and the effect was overpowering. I think I might even have taken a half-step back. But my blinding smile stayed firm.

The only name I remember is Randell and maybe I have that wrong. There was a lot of handshaking and smiling and saying of names. And when all that was done, no one seemed to know what to do. We just stood there, all uncomfortably smiling.

Finally, the man whose name might have been Randell said, "Oh, please, please, sit down," and everyone did.

"Well," Mr. Randell said. "You're a young man to be drawing comics, I must say."

"I've been interested in comics all my life," I said.

"Well, we like your comic very much," he said. "And we'd like to make you an offer for it. Ah, fifteen pounds?"

"I accept," I said.

I don't think Mr. Randell was used to receiving quick decisions, for he then said something that seemed to me enormously ridiculous. "That's, ah, two pounds ten a page," he said, and looked at me with his eyes wide open and one eyebrow higher than the other.

"Yes, that's right," I said. "Six two-and-a-halfs are fifteen. Exactly."

That made his eyes open even wider, and suddenly he shut them altogether and looked down at the floor. One of the other men coughed. No one seemed to know what to do. I leaned back in my chair and crossed my legs and just generally smiled at everyone. I knew what was coming. A job. And I knew what I was going to say then, too.

And then Mr. Randell collected himself, as though he had just thought of something very important (what an actor, I thought) and he said, "Oh, there is one other thing, though. Jim, do we have Mr. Lurie's comic here?"

"Right here," said Jim, and whipped it out from under a pile of things on a desk.

"Some of the, ah, spelling," Mr. Randell said.

"Oh?" I said.

"Well, yes, there are, ah, certain things," he said, turning over the pages of my comic, "not, ah, *big* mistakes, but, here, see? You've spelt it as 'jungel' which is not, ah, common usage."

"You're absolutely right," I said, flashing out my fountain pen all ready to make the correction.

35

"Oh, no no no," Mr. Randell said. "Don't you worry about it. We'll, ah, make the corrections. If you approve, that is."

"Of course," I said.

"We'll, ah, post you our cheque for, ah, fifteen pounds," he said. "In the mail," he added, rather lamely, it seemed to me.

"Oh, there's no great hurry about that," I said. "Any old time at all will do."

"Yes," he said.

Then we fell into another of these silences with which this appointment seemed to be plagued. Mr. Randell scratched his neck. A truck just outside the window started with a roar and then began to whine and grind. It's reversing, I thought. My face felt stiff from smiling, but somehow I couldn't let it go.

Then the man whose name was Jim said, "This is your first comic strip, Mr. Lurie?"

"Yes," I said. My reply snapped across the room like a bullet. I was a little bit embarrassed at its suddenness, but, after all, wasn't this what I had come to talk about?

"It's very professional," he said. "Would you like to see one of our comic strips?"

"Certainly," I said.

He reached down behind the desk and brought out one page of a comic they were running at the moment (I had seen it in the shop when I'd gone to check up on *Boy Magazine*'s address), *The Adventures of Ned Kelly*.

Now, Ned Kelly is all right, but what I like about comics is that they create a world of their own, like, say, *Dick Tracy*, a totally fictitious environment, which any clear-thinking person knows doesn't really exist, and Ned Kelly, well, that was real, it really happened. It wasn't a true comic strip. It was just history in pictures.

But naturally I didn't say any of this to Jim. All I did was lean forward and pretend to study the linework and the inking in and the lettering, which were just so-so, and when I thought I'd done that long enough, I leaned back in my chair and said, "It's very good."

"Jim," said Mr. Randell, who hadn't spoken a word during all this, "maybe you'd like to take Mr. Lurie around and show him the presses. We print *Boy Magazine* right here," he explained to me. "Would you like to see how a magazine is produced?"

"Yes," I said, but the word sounded flat and awful to me. I hated, at thirteen, being shown round things. I still do. How A Great Newspaper Is Produced. How Bottles Are Made. Why Cheese Has Holes And How We Put Them In.

And the rest of it, the job, the core of the matter? But everyone was standing up and Mr. Randell's hand was stretched out to shake mine and Jim was saying, "Follow me," and it was all over.

Now I'm not going to take you through a tour of this factory, the way I was, eating an ice cream which Jim had sent a boy out to buy for me. It lasted for hours. I climbed up where Jim told me to climb up. I looked where he pointed. I nodded when he explained some involved and highly secret process to me. "We use glue, not staples," he explained to me. "Why? Well, it's an economic consideration. Look here," and I looked there, and licked my ice cream and wondered how much more there was of it and was it worth going to school in the afternoon or should I take the whole day off?

But like all things it came to an end. We were at a side door, not the one I had come in through. "Well, nice to meet you," Jim said, and shook my hand. "Find your way back to the station okay? You came by train? It's easy, just follow your nose," and I rode home on the train not caring a damn about how many stations I was going through, not looking out of the window, not even aware of the shortness of the trousers of my ridiculous Good Suit.

Yes, my comic strip appeared and my friends read it and I was a hero for a day at school. My father held the cheque up to the light and said we'd know in a few days if it was any good. My mother didn't say much to me but I heard her on the phone explaining to all her friends what a clever son she had. Clever? That's one word I've never had any time for.

I didn't tell a soul, not even Michael Lazarus, about that awful tour of the factory. I played it very coolly. And a week after my comic strip came out in print, I sat down and drew another comic story and wrapped it up and sent it to them, and this time, I determined, I would do all my business over the phone. With that nice Miss Gordon.

Weeks passed, nearly a whole month. No reply. And then, with a sickening crash, the postman dumped my new comic into our letterbox and flew on his merry way down the street, blowing his whistle and riding his bicycle over everyone's lawns.

There was a letter enclosed with my comic. It said that, unfortunately, *Boy Magazine* was discontinuing publication, and although they enjoyed my comic "enormously," they regretted that they had no option but to return it.

My father had a field day over the whole business but no, no, what's the point of going over all that? Anyhow, I had decided (I told myself) that I didn't want to be a comic-strip artist after all. There was no future in it. It was risky and unsure. It was here today and gone tomorrow. The thing to be was a serious painter, and I set about it at once, spreading new boxes of water colours and tubes of paint all over the dining room table and using every saucer in the house to mix paint. But somehow, right from the start, I knew it was no good. The only thing that was ever real to me I had "grown out of." I had become, like everyone else, a dreamer.

# A LIKELY PLACE

*Paula Fox*

1

Everyone wanted to help Lewis. That's why he was thinking of running away.

But where could he go? He only had thirty-five cents left from his birthday present. His two Canadian dimes didn't count unless he could get as far as Canada.

Lewis was lying in bed watching the reflections of car lights move across his ceiling. He was thinking that if he could just remember the difference between *there* and *their* school wouldn't be so bad, when his mother came into his room.

"Are you still awake, Lewis?" she asked.

"Sort of," he said.

"Is there something on your mind, dear?"

What *was* on his mind? Lewis wondered. Skin, then brownish hair, then a woolen cap he had taken to wearing even when the weather was warm.

"Why, Lewis! You're still wearing that hat!" his mother exclaimed. "In bed, Lewis!"

"I forgot to take it off," he answered, which was only half true. He didn't especially want to explain that wearing the hat made him feel everything inside his head was in the right place.

"Well . . ." his mother said, hesitating at the door, "I think you should try to sleep."

He listened to his mother's footsteps going on down the hall, then he got up and walked over to his fish tank. The fish had been supplied by his parents to give him something to take care of so he could become responsible. They bored him to death.

When Lewis awoke the next morning, his youngest cousin was sitting on his bed. Lewis knew it must be Saturday. One Saturday every month his uncle and aunt and cousin came to visit.

"Where'd you get that hat?" asked his cousin.

"It's just a hat," said Lewis.

"A sleeping hat," said the cousin.

Lewis got up and began to get dressed. His clothes were in a heap where he had left them. His cousin watched as Lewis untangled a shoelace from a belt buckle and a shirt sleeve from a pants leg.

"You'll probably end up at Charlie Flocker's Farm," his cousin said.

"What's that?" asked Lewis.

"Oh, a place for people who hang their clothes on the floor and who sit down and don't do anything all day," replied the cousin.

41

"Who told you that?" asked Lewis.

"My mother told me," said his cousin. "And her mother told her, and her mother's mother—"

"Stop!" shouted Lewis. "Just tell me, what do they do there?"

The cousin crossed his eyes.

Lewis considered asking his own mother about Charlie Flocker. Probably she would say, "Oh, Lewis!" and give him an oatmeal cookie.

Lewis and his cousin went off to the kitchen to get some breakfast. His aunt and uncle and mother and father were drinking coffee at the kitchen table. They all looked up.

"I found the slipper you lost last month, Lewis," said his mother. "It was under the refrigerator."

"Lewis, do you have a plan for those batteries which are soaking in your spare fishbowl?" asked his father. "Because if you don't, I'll just remove them. A pity to stain the glass so."

That morning he and his cousin were taken to the museum. It was one of many places Lewis was taken to, even when he didn't care to go: the zoo, the playground, the beach, plays, concerts, ballets, museums.

Lewis' cousin found a big glass case full of swords. While they were deciding which ones they would like to have, Lewis' aunt called out, "Lewis, do look at this nice little sphinx! Imagine! It's three thousand years old!"

Then his mother called out, "Lewis, come and see this statue of a Roman senator. Doesn't it look like your uncle?"

He wondered why they left his cousin alone. Maybe it was because his cousin was still little. Lewis leaned up against a column until a museum guard scowled and motioned to him to move. His father hurried over.

"Are you all right?" asked his father.

"Fine," said Lewis. If he could have one wish it would be to make people stop asking him how he felt—or telling him how he felt. "You must feel embarrassed because you spell so poorly," his teacher would say. "You must feel lonely on a rainy day like this with no one to play with," a friend of his mother would say. "It's too bad you live in the city where you only have a dirty, dinky playground to run around in," an absolute stranger would say. Lewis could have made a list a mile long of all the things people had told him he was feeling.

Just before his aunt and uncle left the museum to go home, his cousin whispered to him, "If you have a book and act like you're reading it, it's easier."

That night he took a book from the shelf, and while he was lying in bed looking at it, a hand turned it over to see the title. It was his mother's hand, but his father's voice said, "Hm . . . well . . . I see . . . uh-huh . . . well, well!"

Lewis spent most of Sunday thinking about running away. He wondered if anyone guessed. The doorman of the building across the street always seemed to be watching for him. He had heard of mind readers. Maybe the doorman was one.

His mother and father were walking back and forth in the living room exchanging sections of the Sunday paper. Lewis went out on the service stairs of the building to play solitaire. He liked it on the stairs. When the handymen who fixed things ran up and down from floor to floor.

the noise was thunderous but Lewis didn't mind. The
King of Hearts in his deck of cards had a large sooty heel
print where one of the handymen had stepped on it.
He could have erased the print with his gum eraser if
he hadn't lost it.

The next morning as he passed the doorman on his
way to catch the school bus, the doorman called out,
"Hello, kid. That's the ticket, kid! Get yourself educated!"

Why would the doorman say that to him, Lewis
asked himself, unless he suspected that Lewis was up
to something? Something like running away?

When he got to school, Lewis suddenly remembered
the test the class was having the first thing that morning.
But he had forgotten the name of the capital of Honduras.
He stood in the corridor, knowing he had been marked
absent. He was leaning against the wall, trying to think
what to do, when the school principal walked up and put
his arm around his shoulders.

"Lewis, you should be in class," he said.

"I know it," Lewis replied.

"We are trying to help children, Lewis," said the
principal. "But they have to try, too. Isn't that so?"

Lewis had heard some other questions like that one. "It's
raining out, isn't it?" or "It's time for you to go to bed, isn't
it?" or "Tomatoes are good for you, aren't they?" If he said
*no* to any of these questions, grownups would look dizzy.

The principal led Lewis into the classroom. The
principal smiled at the teacher, who smiled back. Lewis
didn't smile at anybody. He couldn't even remember
where Honduras was.

When he got home that afternoon, his mother said she had something to tell him. In a few days, she said, it would be May, time for the annual trip to Chicago to visit relatives.

"We'll only be gone for a week," she said.

"Okay," said Lewis.

"You'll like Miss Fitchlow who is going to take care of you," she said.

"All right," said Lewis.

"Next year, we might even take you," his mother said. "If your schoolwork gets better."

He started for his room.

"Oh, Lewis, your three friends are waiting for you. Outside on the service stairs."

Lewis was glad to hear they were there and ran to the hall closet to get the old army blanket for them to sit on, because the stairs were cold. If they got cold they wouldn't stay to hear the ghost stories he read to them.

"Lewis! Wait!" his mother said. "How old are Henry and Betty Anne and Thomas?"

"Different ages," said Lewis.

"Oh, Lewis! I mean their average age."

"They're all around seven," Lewis answered.

"And you're going to be ten soon," his mother said. "Don't you think they're a little young for you? Wouldn't you rather play with children your own age?"

Lewis shrugged. He knew his mother was smiling only because she wanted him to do something different from what he was going to do.

"Are your friends all the same age?" he asked.

"That's not polite, Lewis," his mother replied.

"I was only asking," he said.

He did like to read to the children. They often waited for him in the afternoon. Henry usually had an apple and Betty Anne and Thomas had a box of animal crackers. Until his eyes got used to the light in the service stairs he could hardly see anything except their eyes. They reminded him of a family of pandas. They each sat on their own step, squinched up against the wall, looking to see which book he had brought with him. The only objection he had to reading to them was that they liked to hear the same story over and over again. He had read *The Monkey's Paw* a dozen times. They particularly liked him to screech or moan or squeak like a door with rusty hinges at the exciting parts.

When Lewis' mother called out from the kitchen to see if everyone was all right, Henry shouted back, "Super!" Lewis wished he could get the hang of answering grown-ups. It seemed to him that everyone knew how to manage this problem except him.

On Tuesday, at school, the whole class had a recorder lesson. But Lewis had to have an extra one. He hadn't yet learned the school song or the special piece his class was to play on their recorders for assembly. Miss Mowdith, the music teacher, said that Lewis was throwing the whole class off key.

"I think, Lewis," she said, "that you must be hearing the music of outer space. I never heard a G like that in my entire life! My dear boy! If we could amplify that note of yours over a public-address system, all the mice living in this city would hit the road!"

So that afternoon Lewis went to Miss Mowdith's apartment for his special lesson. The two rooms were filled with musical instruments. Even in the kitchen, there were piccolos. A blue-eyed cat was sitting on a harpsichord.

"The cat bites people," Miss Mowdith said as Lewis reached up a hand to pet it.

Then Lewis played his G. The cat jumped a foot in the air and ran for cover.

"Oh!" exclaimed Miss Mowdith. "What shall we ever do with you?"

That, Lewis gathered, was the problem. Even Henry had complained yesterday that Lewis' screeches weren't as scary as they used to be.

On Thursday he handed in his weekly composition, and no sooner had his teacher looked at it than she dropped it on her desk.

"Lewis, you must learn to spell *their*. What will happen to you if you can't tell the difference between *there* and *their*?"

What *would* happen? Lewis wondered, as he wrote *their* fifty times. He was writing out the words so they formed a design like a snake on the lined paper. The teacher looked over his shoulder. "Lewis, you must learn the difference between a drawing class and a spelling exercise."

He put a note on the teacher's desk in which he wrote that her elbows looked like clam shells. He didn't sign it, but she seemed to know whom it was from.

"Not everyone in this world can have beautiful elbows," she said to him that afternoon.

That evening his father, who had heard about Lewis' spelling difficulties, said, "I should think a ten-year-old boy would be able to spell *their*."

"I'm nine," said Lewis.

"Going on ten," said his father. "Maybe I can help you."

But Lewis spelled *their* instantly and correctly.

"Any other words bothering you?" asked his father as he picked up Lewis' marbles from the living room floor and handed them to him.

"Not yet," said Lewis.

"That's not what I heard," said his father.

"Heard," repeated Lewis, "H-E-A-R-D."

"All right, Lewis. That will do!" said his father.

Lewis would have liked Fridays to disappear from the week. But then, he supposed, he would have to have the weekly spelling test on Thursday. But to his surprise he spelled *their* correctly that morning. The teacher announced to the class that Lewis had, at last, learned the word. Lewis felt rather good about the whole thing except that he wished his classmates hadn't clapped so loudly.

Later his teacher took him aside, reminding him that the spring reports would be due soon. She asked him what he was really interested in.

"Pygmies," said Lewis.

"Don't be funny," she said. Lewis looked down at his shoes. He had drawn a face on the toe of one with a marking pen. It was his right shoe. He had trouble remembering which was right and which was left. The face reminded him.

"Perhaps you're serious," the teacher said. "Would you like to make your report on pygmies? We're delighted you're interested in something."

Pygmies did interest him. He had seen a picture of a pygmy bridge in a magazine. It had been made from vines and then slung over a stream somewhere in Africa. There were several pygmies standing in the middle of the bridge with their arms around one another. They were all smiling.

"Could I do a report on something else?" Lewis asked. He wanted to keep the pygmies for himself. He didn't care to write all about the population of the pygmies or what they ate and what they learned in school or how they made a living. He didn't want to cut out and paste pictures of pygmies on white paper and put a cover around his report and read it to the class.

The teacher sighed. "Well . . . Do a report on something," she said.

That very evening his father asked him what he liked best.

"A pygmy bridge," Lewis said, because it had been on his mind all day.

His father sighed too. "I don't understand you, Lewis," he said. His mother gave him a cookie and said they would bring him back a nice present from Chicago.

That's the way things were with Lewis.

As soon as it was May the weather seemed to change and grow warmer. Cats came out from behind garbage cans and wandered down the streets. The trees began to bloom. The doorman across the street unbuttoned his jacket, leaned against the wall, and went to sleep standing up. Young flies flew through the classroom, and a bee crawled in one morning and swooped across the desks while all the girls screamed.

Lewis' mother and father would soon be leaving for Chicago.

"A little change of routine," his father said. "It'll be a change for you, too, Lewis," he added.

Lewis wasn't interested in going to Chicago but he didn't want to stay home either. He hadn't met Miss Fitchlow yet. His mother said she was very nice. What could that mean? He hoped she wouldn't be like some of the other baby-sitters he had had. Mrs. Carmichael, for instance, had worn fat, purple slippers and had followed him around all day, and had even sat next to his bed at night until he had pretended to fall asleep. Mrs. Carmichael had hummed to herself all day long, always just one note. Perhaps that's where he had learned his special G.

Or Miss Fitchlow might be like Jake Elderberry, who sat on evenings when his parents went to the movies, and whose hair fell over his eyes and who thought he saw things behind the curtains. Or worst of all, she might be like Miss Bender, who weighed all the food she intended to eat on a little scale, and who washed everything a hundred times and who practically fell out the window scaring away the birds because, she said, they carried deadly germs in their feathers.

On Saturday morning while his parents were packing, Lewis went out for a walk. The sun was warm. He passed many baby carriages and children on tricycles. At the entrance to the park he saw dozens of dogs running around with their ears and tails up. They looked very busy. As he was watching them, he noticed a fat woman walking right toward him. She wobbled.

"Hello, honey," she said. "Knock 'em dead!" she added seriously, and her words ran together as though the sun was melting them.

He stared at her as she passed him and wobbled on down the street. Then, because he wanted to see what she would do next, he ran after her until people began to look at him and scowl.

"Running boys should do without their suppers!" croaked an old man, waving his cane at Lewis as he ran by. Finally he couldn't see the lady anymore. He went back to the park entrance. He hadn't been in the park without his father or his mother. In another year, his father said, he would be allowed to go by himself if he had gotten to be a responsible boy by that time. It was, after all, a very big park. Lewis couldn't even see over the trees to the other side, where the river was. There was a zoo in it somewhere. There were lakes and paths and big rocks. Lewis thought that there must be a cave or two. He hoped he might be able to live in one for a while.

When he got back to the apartment, his parents were standing in the hall with their suitcases beside them. A tall, thin lady with a freckled face and reddish hair was there with them.

"This is Miss Fitchlow, Lewis," said his mother. "She has our number."

Miss Fitchlow laughed. She sounded like a horse. Lewis noticed his mother looked quickly at his father. Then his parents hugged him and reminded him of all the things he needed and all the things he should do as well as all the things he shouldn't do. Then they left.

"Say, pal, you've got a face on your left shoe," said Miss Fitchlow as they were standing in the hall.

"It's on my right shoe," Lewis said.

"Right you are!" Miss Fitchlow cried. "I ought to know that by now. Come with me! I'll show you something."

Lewis followed her into the living room, where Miss Fitchlow sank down instantly to the floor, her feet arranged in a peculiar way, crossed, each foot pointing straight up.

"Lotus position," she said. "Keep your back straight. Breathe deeply. Be quiet about it. Think nothing. Marvelous for the appetite. Do you like yogurt? Some hate it. I brought my own brand. You can try it. Also pumpkin seeds. But honey is the greatest! What's the matter? Can't get your legs crossed? What do you expect? It takes time to learn, like everything else."

Lewis fell over backwards.

"What's this for besides appetite?" Lewis asked.

"Anything at all," Miss Fitchlow replied.

He ate a chop for dinner. Miss Fitchlow sloshed around a

big bowl of yogurt. It tasted queer to him—like undecided milk.

"How about some nuts?" she asked.

They ate nuts until there was a big pile of shells on the kitchen table.

"Something on your mind?" she asked. "So have I." But she didn't ask him what it was, or tell him what she was thinking about.

He decided to ask her a question he had been turning over for a week or so.

"Did you ever hear of Charlie Flocker?" he asked.

She rested her chin on her hand. "Charlie Flocker? Let's see. Say, I knew a Charlie Flocker in Bombay. He was there to study the rope trick. I don't think he ever could manage it. It's pretty tough to just disappear."

"Bombay?" asked Lewis.

"India," she said.

"He runs a farm," Lewis said.

"Not the Charlie I knew," said Miss Fitchlow. "He couldn't run a scooter."

"Maybe there're two of them," said Lewis.

"Possible, but not probable," said Miss Fitchlow.

"He runs this place for people who don't do anything," Lewis said.

"That's for me!" shouted Miss Fitchlow and laughed her horse laugh. Then she began to wash the dishes.

"I hate to dry," she said. "You dry, pal."

"I don't know how," Lewis said.

She handed him a wet plate and a towel. "Figure it out," she said.

He dropped one fork and when it clanged on the kitchen floor, Miss Fitchlow did a little dancing, snapping her fingers together and rolling her eyes.

The next morning Lewis found Miss Fitchlow in the living room lying between two chairs, her feet on one, her head on the other, the rest of her in-between.

"Pretty good, eh?" she said. "Took me years to learn this one. You can start your breakfast. I have another two minutes to go before I can get up."

Lewis went to the kitchen but there was nothing on the table. He drank a whole can of apricot juice and toasted an English muffin, which he ate with peanut butter on it.

"How was it?" asked Miss Fitchlow from the door. She looked a little taller. He wondered if her morning exercise had stretched her.

"It was okay," said Lewis.

"What have you in mind for today?" she asked.

"I thought I'd go to the park," he said, hoping his parents hadn't told Miss Fitchlow he wasn't responsible yet.

"Pretty good," she said. "Cover the peanut butter. It'll get dry as a bone. No point in that."

He did.

"Not that fresh peanuts aren't better," she added.

The dogs in the park were not so busy today. Some of them were asleep, stretched out beneath the trees with their tails curled around them so they looked like neat packages. Lewis walked through the entrance. He would have been worried if he hadn't been so excited. He could just imagine his father smiling as he said, "Why, Lewis! Don't you remember that we asked you not to go into the park?"

Then he saw a small snake curling through the grass. He leaped for it. It wound itself around his wrist. A lady who was passing by uttered a little screech and hurried on. A man walked up to him.

"What have you there?" he asked.

"A snake," said Lewis.

"So I see," the man said, "but one must do better than that. It is known as DeKay's snake. Notice the chestnut color. Note the black dots along its sides."

The snake slid off Lewis' arm and disappeared beneath a bush.

"Easy come, easy go," said the man. Lewis walked on.

Everything in the world seemed to have a name.

He came to a fork in the path and, looking down at his shoes, turned right. Soon he came to a small square enclosed by trees, with benches all around a few yards of gravel. An old man was sitting alone on a bench. He wore a high, black hat and had on gloves. There was a large umbrella furled across his lap. Lewis observed him for a while. The old man was talking to himself. Although he spoke in a loud, clear voice, the words were in a language which Lewis didn't understand.

A boy zipped through the square on a bicycle. Lewis jumped back. The old man looked up.

"Too fast!" said the old man. "Square wheels would have changed history." Lewis wasn't sure to whom he was speaking.

"You got a bicycle, too?" asked the old man. Lewis looked around quickly. But there was no one in the square except himself and the old man. He shook his head.

"I only wish I had such a bicycle," the old man said, sighing. "I'd ride it like a devil. Ride it, ride it all the way home!"

Lewis looked at the umbrella so the old man couldn't tell that he was surprised.

"Who can tell?" said the old man. "It might rain."

Another mind reader, thought Lewis, and he started to leave the square.

"Wait!" cried the old man. "Don't you want to know where my home is? Have you no curiosity?"

Lewis halted. If he walked away, the old man might ask him where he was going. He might even tell him he shouldn't be in the park.

"Barcelona!" shouted the old man. "And I'll tell you something. If I could ride a bicycle in the first place, I could ride it across the Atlantic Ocean in the second place."

"Is that the capital of Honduras?" Lewis asked.

"Honduras!" exclaimed the old man. "Barcelona in Honduras," he repeated as if astonished. "Why—it's in Spain, dear friend. Come over here and sit down. I must tell you a thing or two."

Lewis sat down on the bench next to the old man.

"It is a large city, very splendid, on the Mediterranean Sea. Ships come to its harbor from all over the world, even from Honduras. In the middle of the streets there are *ramblas*. On those splendid *ramblas* a person can walk at any time of the day or night and nobody will knock him down with a car. In the afternoons after my work was done, I had a cup of chocolate so thick it had to be eaten with a spoon. Often I think to myself—what has happened,

Emilio? Boys on bicycles make my brains rattle, and instead of chocolate in the afternoons, I sit here on this bench and try to compose myself and write a letter, and when it is too cold to sit here, I sit in my room and try to write this same letter."

"Who are you writing to?" asked Lewis.

The old man scowled. "To my son-in-law who married my daughter, Preciosa."

"Where does he live?" asked Lewis.

"In the same house I am," replied the old man.

"Can't you just tell him?" Lewis asked.

"Can you tell a rock? No! I will write. Then I must go home to Barcelona," said the old man.

"All right," said Lewis.

"It's all wrong," said the old man. "I been here three years. Observe my English! Beautiful! But I can't write it. What kind of mad language is it? You see a word and it's nothing like the way you say it. Sometimes I jump up and down on the newspapers and Preciosa comes running and explains to me the stupid word I cannot understand because of this crazy spelling. The sound and the writing are not even cousins. In my language, it's intelligent. My name is Madruga. Spell it!"

"Me?" asked Lewis.

"You," said the old man.

Lewis spelled it.

"Perfect! You see?" asked the old man. "Even a person who does not speak can spell. What is your name?"

"Lewis."

The old man spelled: "L-U-I-S."

"No," said Lewis.

"Try another," said the old man.

"Cough," said Lewis.

"Ah!" exclaimed the old man. "Watch! C-O-F."

"Wrong," said Lewis.

"Naturally," said the old man. "Because it is unreasonable, English. What can you expect?"

"Where did you have the chocolate?" asked Lewis.

"In the café," said the old man. "At a table beneath a small umbrella, out on the sidewalk where I could watch the people walking pleasantly on the *ramblas*. But now I have neither chocolate nor work. My son-in-law won't permit me. I am extraordinarily skilled. I make beautiful shoes, everything by hand. But he says I drop things. I have never dropped anything in my life. He says, 'Go read the newspapers.' What is in the newspapers? News. Nothing."

"What do you do?" asked Lewis.

"I come to the park and sit on this bench and think about this letter which I cannot write. I sit and sit. Then I go home and sit in my room. Then it is supper at a barbaric hour, 5:30. My son-in-law doesn't eat. How can he? He is watching me all the time. 'Pa,' he says, 'you are about to drop your spoon.' "

"What's his name?" asked Lewis.

"Charlie," replied the old man, looking sad.

"Charlie Flocker?" asked Lewis.

"What's that?" asked the old man.

"Nothing," said Lewis. Then he asked, "What's the letter for?"

"For telling Charlie what I think. Also my plans. He thinks I am too old to have plans," replied the old man.

They were silent for a little while.

"I suppose," the old man said at last, "that you can write this insane language, English?"

"Sometimes," said Lewis.

"Ah, I understand," said the old man. "It is like having fits, no?"

Lewis nodded.

"Would you do me the great favor of writing this letter?" asked the old man. He looked at Lewis with a serious expression. "I will tell it to you," he said, "and you will spell."

"Okay," said Lewis. "But I make mistakes."

"Think nothing of it," said the old man. "Could we begin now? I have paper and pencil in my pocket."

"I was going to look for a cave," said Lewis.

The old man looked disappointed.

"But I can do it tomorrow," said Lewis.

"I am very good at caves," said the old man eagerly. "And I can help you. That will be in exchange for the letter."

"All right," Lewis said.

The old man reached into his pocket and took out a pad of paper and a short yellow pencil.

"My esteemed son-in-law Charles," he began.

Lewis looked up at him. "How about 'Dear Charlie'?" he asked.

"Ah, that's better," said the old man. "Customs are different everywhere. Now, write: 'Sometimes I ask myself

59

what am I? An old chair to gather dust in the corner? Me? A skilled shoemaker?' "

"Wait!" said Lewis. "You're going too fast."

The old man folded his hands over his umbrella and waited until Lewis was finished writing.

"Here's what I wrote," said Lewis shortly. "'Dear Charlie, I don't want to sit in a corner. I want to make some shoes.'"

The old man smiled for the first time. A gold tooth shone in his mouth. "Very good," he said. "Now—"

But he was interrupted by the appearance in the square of a large man in a green jacket. Lewis wondered whose hat he was wearing. It couldn't have been his own.

"Pa!" cried the man. "Pressy's got a big Sunday dinner all ready and here you are, stuck to that bench as usual. The spuds are burned and the peas are as hard as pebbles. Come on home now before something else happens!"

The old man whispered to Lewis behind his hand. "You heard? *Pressy!* My poor daughter!"

"Move, Pa!" said the man. "You ought to play with people your own age!"

The old man shouted rapidly in the same language Lewis had heard him speak when he first came to the square.

"Cut the cackle!" said Charlie. "Let's make time!"

The old man rose slowly to his feet and bowed to Lewis. "Perhaps we can continue tomorrow," he said gravely.

"It has to be later because of school," Lewis explained.

"At your convenience," said the old man.

"Pa!" bawled the large man.

"After three," Lewis said hurriedly.

"I will be here with the nothing newspaper," said the old man, and he twirled his umbrella and began to walk away.

*"Adiós,"* he called back over his shoulder.

When Lewis walked into his apartment, Miss Fitchlow was standing on her head in a corner of the hall.

"Good for the brains," she said.


3


Lewis looked at the classroom clock only twice during the day. Each time, he was surprised to see how far the hour hand had advanced.

It was a strange Monday. He hardly knew he was in school because he was thinking so hard about old Mr. Madruga and about how he must finish all his work so he would not be kept in after school.

While he was looking up the word "shoemaker" in the classroom dictionary (in case he should have to use it in Mr. Madruga's letter), he found a number of other words he had not seen before. He learned, for example, that "shoo" was a sound used to frighten birds away, and that a "shogun" was a Japanese ruler.

"Why, Lewis!" cried his teacher. "You're using the dictionary!"

Lewis muttered "shoo!" under his breath.

"What?" asked the teacher.

"Spanish is easier to spell," he said.

"So it is," she agreed.

"What's your hurry, kid?" shouted the doorman as Lewis raced past him on his way home.

Miss Fitchlow was in the kitchen making carrot pudding.

"In case you want to see in the dark," said Miss Fitchlow, pointing to the pudding, "this guarantees it. Takes a bit of getting used to, though. How about a taste?"

"Wow!" said Lewis after he had taken a bite.

He waited for her to ask him what had happened in school. Perhaps she didn't really know where he had been most of the day.

"I was in school," he said.

"Ah!" said Miss Fitchlow. "The old daily double."

"I've got to go to the park now," he said.

"Okay," said Miss Fitchlow.

"What are you going to do?" Lewis asked.

"Meditate," she replied.

"What's that?" he asked.

"Clean out the attic," she said.

He thought about attics all the way to the square in the park. He thought of trunks and spider webs and old birdcages, the kind he had seen in his cousin's attic. Miss Fitchlow reminded him of agreeable things even though he didn't always understand what she was talking about.

Mr. Madruga was sitting on the same bench, his umbrella resting between his knees, a folded newspaper beside him. Lewis thought he was asleep. Then the old man looked up.

"Oho!" said Mr. Madruga. "My dear friend, I've made you something." He held out a bird made from newspaper.

It was very small and had many paper feathers. It rested lightly on Lewis' palm.

"Thank you," he said.

"It's nothing," said the old man. "First, we will look for a cave."

Lewis was happy because Mr. Madruga had remembered.

They walked away from the square and down a path. They passed a duck pond. The ducks were gathered around an old lady, through whose fingers grains of corn trickled.

"My ducks!" she cried as they walked by.

"Splendid!" said Mr. Madruga loudly. He whispered to Lewis, "Personally, I don't care for ducks."

The path they were following wound up a hill. At the top, where there were no trees, only a few gray rocks, they found a man staring up at the sun. They watched him a minute.

"What are you doing, please?" asked Mr. Madruga politely.

"I'm teaching myself to look at the sun," the man said.

"I can see the sun," Lewis said.

"No, you can't," said the man. "No one can see it. It's much too bright. But in a few days, I will be able to see it. Then I'll write a book. I'll call it, 'The Sun and I.' Or even better, 'I and the Sun.' " Suddenly he turned to look at them. "I can't see you yet," he said. "If you wait a minute until my eyes adjust, I'll describe my plan to you."

Mr. Madruga and Lewis tiptoed down the other side of the hill. When they looked back, the man had resumed his former position and was staring straight up at the sky.

"Can you see the sun?" asked Lewis.

"In a way," replied Mr. Madruga. "But I prefer to see the ground." Then he cried, "Look out for the infants!"

Just in time, Lewis saw two babies crawling at high speed directly toward him. Behind them, huffing and panting, came a lady in a white uniform.

"Gertrude! Matthew! This is positively the worst you've ever been. Come back! Come back at once!" she cried.

But the babies kept right on going, so Lewis had to jump off the path to get out of their way.

"Devils!" muttered the lady as she passed them. Mr. Madruga was laughing so hard that he had to lean on his umbrella. Lewis began to laugh too.

"Maybe they'll escape," he said.

"No, no," said Mr. Madruga, wiping his eyes. "They won't escape. But they go very fast, no?"

"Will we find a cave soon?" asked Lewis.

"In time," said Mr. Madruga. "An empty cave is the most difficult thing of all to find." Then he turned off the path, holding back the branches of some thick bushes so that Lewis could follow him.

"Why are we going here?" asked Lewis.

"It's a likely place," answered Mr. Madruga.

How different the park looked here! No paths, no baskets for litter, no benches, no people. It was almost like the country. They walked through a small meadow of fresh spring grass. Ahead of them was another hill, but this one had no paths, and the rock faces were steep and smooth. Lewis ran ahead. Almost immediately he saw a cave opening. It was dark and jagged but wide enough even for Mr. Madruga. Lewis peered inside.

"Occupied!" shouted a voice.

"Inhabited!" shouted another.

"Positively filled to capacity!" cried a third.

Lewis sprang back.

"That was full," he reported to Mr. Madruga, who had waited for him in the meadow.

"There will be more," said Mr. Madruga.

The next cave was too small for Lewis to get his head in and look around. The third cave was full of water. "For that one," said Mr. Madruga, "we would need a boat."

"We'll never find one," said Lewis, feeling discouraged.

"There!" said Mr. Madruga, pointing with his umbrella right in front of them. All Lewis could see was a tangle of vines.

"Lift them!" said the old man. Lewis pushed the vines away.

"What have you found?" asked Mr. Madruga.

"A big, empty cave," said Lewis.

It was large enough at the entrance for both of them to enter at the same time. There was a low ledge near the entrance upon which Mr. Madruga spread his newspaper. He sat down and waited while Lewis explored the cave.

Ten long strides took Lewis to the back wall. There he found a candle stub stuck into a soup can. He also found one black shoe with its laces. He must remember to look for someone wearing only one shoe on his way home. Underneath some dead leaves, he found a small, slightly damp booklet. The title was *Mosquito Control in Southeastern Delaware*.

Lewis returned to Mr. Madruga with the candle and the booklet.

Mr. Madruga took a kitchen match from his pocket and after lighting it with his thumbnail, lit the candle. Then he took out the notebook in which Lewis had started the letter to Charlie yesterday. Lewis put the paper bird down on the ledge between them.

They didn't really need the candle, because daylight was pouring in through the mouth of the cave. But it was nice to see the flame flicker in the light breeze.

"Shall we continue?" asked Mr. Madruga.

"Ready," said Lewis.

"You are content with your cave?" asked Mr. Madruga.

"Yes," said Lewis.

"In my country," said Mr. Madruga, "only the best dancers and the best singers live in caves."

"With furniture?" asked Lewis.

"With everything. Everything," answered the old man. Then he said, "Use the book you found for a little desk."

Lewis held up the pencil to show he was ready.

"Without work, I am nothing, nothing, an empty valise!" cried Mr. Madruga. "Charlie! You have stopped me from looking for work. You tell me to 'take it easy,' and I ask myself, what does this mean—"

"Wait!" cried Lewis.

"I was carried away by my feelings," explained Mr. Madruga.

"Is this all right?" asked Lewis after thinking and writing a few minutes. Then he read, " 'You won't let me look for work.' "

"Yes, yes," said Mr. Madruga. "He even says I must not carry my umbrella. He says it's old-fashioned. Is rain old-fashioned? Also, it is pleasant to lean on. Imagine! He puts food into my mouth, turns out my light at night, and holds my arm when we walk as if I were going to fall down on my knees!"

Mr. Madruga stood up and flourished his umbrella. The cave was not high enough for him to stand straight. Soon he calmed down again.

"Tell him," he said, "that I intend to go back to my own country as soon as I can find a ship. Tell him I would rather live in a cave with the gypsies dancing and singing and keeping me up all night than in his house. Also say thank you for his trouble and the many toothbrushes he has bought me while I have lived here."

After Lewis had finished the letter, he read it back to Mr. Madruga. It read:

*Dear Charlie,*

*I don't want to sit in the corner. I want to make some shoes. You won't let me look for work. I am going home to Spain to live in a cave and stay up all night. Thank you for the toothbrushes.*

"Excellent!" said Mr. Madruga. "You have the English style. The Spanish style is also very pretty. Now put 'With many wishes for your continued good health, I am always your obedient servant,' and then I will sign my name."

"Could you just say 'goodbye'?" asked Lewis.

Mr. Madruga looked disappointed.

"I can't spell all those words," Lewis explained.

"In that case, yes. Put 'goodbye.' But in Spanish. *Adiós.* You can spell that?"

"Is this right?" asked Lewis, after thinking awhile.

"Of course," said Mr. Madruga. "But a little mark is required over the 'o' for emphasis."

Then Mr. Madruga signed his name, which took almost two entire lines.

"Is that just one name?" asked Lewis.

"Yes. It is nice to have such a name. When I am melancholy, I say my name over to myself and sometimes I feel cheerful again. *Emilio del Camino de Herrera de Santiago Martinez y Madruga.*"

The candle went out.

"Will you hand him the letter?" asked Lewis.

"No," replied Mr. Madruga. "I will leave the table after the soup. I will put the letter next to his plate. Then I will go to my room and wait until he has read it."

"Will you come to the park tomorrow?"

"If not tomorrow, then the next day. Then I will tell you the news. Who knows what will happen? I may be put out on the street like an old table. In that case, of course, I will defend myself with the umbrella!"

Lewis buried the remains of the candle in a pile of leaves at the back of the cave. He poked the mosquito book in a crack in the wall. He placed the paper bird on a little projecting shelf, where the wind could not blow it away.

"*Adiós,*" Lewis said to Mr. Madruga.

"*Adiós, amigo,*" replied Mr. Madruga.

After supper that evening, Miss Fitchlow told Lewis a story about an owl who chased a mouse all over the world, through jungles and cities, across deserts and mountains, flying, riding on the masts of ships, even hiding in freight cars.

"Why did the owl want that special mouse?" asked Lewis.

"He had an *idée fixe*," said Miss Fitchlow.

"What's that?" Lewis asked.

"An idea that a person, or a bird, can't get rid of," explained Miss Fitchlow. She said that by the time the owl had caught up with the mouse, the mouse had become a plump, smart, giant mouse, very strong in the legs because of all the running it had had to do to escape the owl.

"Then what happened?" asked Lewis.

"Nothing much," said Miss Fitchlow.

"Did he eat it?" Lewis asked.

"Did who eat what?" she asked.

"The owl eat the mouse?"

"The owl gave up mice and rats and became a vegetarian," said Miss Fitchlow.

"Why?"

"Discretion is the better part of valor," said Miss Fitchlow, "which means that if your dinner is bigger and tougher than you are, you'd better change your diet."

"Oh," said Lewis.

"I feel a cartwheel coming on," said Miss Fitchlow. "Make way!"

And with that, she did a double cartwheel across the living room floor.

## 4

Mr. Madruga was not in the park Tuesday or Wednesday or Thursday. At first, Lewis was very disappointed. Perhaps Mr. Madruga hadn't liked the letter Lewis had written for him. Perhaps he had just forgotten about him.

Of course, Charlie might have given him errands to do or might have made him read all the newspapers. Charlie might have decided he didn't want Mr. Madruga to go to the park anymore. Or else the old man might have found a ship to take him home. Perhaps he was, even now, drinking his chocolate in a café and watching people walk on the *ramblas*.

Still, Lewis had his cave.

Every afternoon, after he had checked the square to make sure Mr. Madruga was not there, Lewis went to the cave. Wednesday, he had seen another DeKay's snake near the entrance and had wondered if it was the same one he had seen his first day in the park.

Miss Fitchlow had been starchy about matches so he was unable to light the candle—not that he really needed it.

"Fire is sacred, my boy," Miss Fitchlow had said. "Like most sacred things, it tends to get easily out of hand."

Lewis had a good time in the cave, although he missed Mr. Madruga. He furnished it with a shoebox for interesting stones and bottle tops, a box of saltines in case he got hungry, along with several handfuls of nuts Miss Fitchlow had given him, and the blanket he had used for reading to the children on the service stairs. The bird was still on the ledge, although its paper feathers had wilted a little.

To pass the time, he read the booklet about mosquitoes in Delaware. He thought maybe he could use it for a report for the class.

He wondered if he could stand on his head without Miss Fitchlow there to catch him if he fell over. He smoothed out a place on the dirt floor of the cave and covered it with leaves. The first time he tried he fell on his face. The second time he managed to get himself up, his legs straight and pointed up at the cave's roof. Then he let himself down in sections like a telescope and assumed the lotus position, breathing deeply. After that he felt quite light-headed.

On Thursday a small dog wandered into the cave. It was extremely friendly and it ate a number of peanuts from Lewis' hand. On the dog's collar tag Lewis read: "My name is Myra. I belong to Mr. Klopper."

"Myra," said Lewis. The dog wagged her tail.

"I bet somebody is following you," Lewis said. "I bet you're not even supposed to be in the park."

Myra wagged her tail.

"Say something," said Lewis.

Myra gave a low bark.

"I can spell anything," Lewis said. "Even that!"

Myra barked again.

"R-O-O-F," Lewis spelled. "Don't you know any other words? You're not responsible, Myra, old dog. You shouldn't be allowed out without a keeper. Take a letter, Myra. Ready? 'Dear Mr. Klopper, you shouldn't smile at Myra when you want her to stop doing something like chewing up the rug. Just tell her. Also, don't wake her up in the middle of the night to ask her what she's thinking about. It will make her have stiff brains.' "

Myra jumped up and licked Lewis' chin.

"Calm yourself," Lewis said sternly.

Myra drifted away after she and Lewis had finished the peanuts. It was pleasant to have guests dropping in.

After Myra left, Lewis began to feel sad again thinking about Mr. Madruga and wondering where he was. He tried saying the old man's name over to himself, but he could only remember half of it.

He went home earlier that afternoon. He walked up the service stairs thinking that maybe he'd find Henry or Thomas or Betty Anne to read to, but he only found Henry sitting outside his own door with an apple core in one hand.

"You don't read to us anymore," Henry said reproachfully.

"I have other things to do than read to you all the time," Lewis said. "Anyhow, you ought to learn to read yourself."

"I can read," Henry said in a sulky voice. "But I want to hear about the monkey's paw."

"You have heard about that a thousand times," Lewis said. "Read it yourself."

"I'll get somebody else to read it to me," Henry said.

"You're just a silly little kid," said Lewis crossly. Henry popped the apple core in his mouth and made a face at Lewis.

Lewis ran up to his own floor.

"I want to hear about that monkey," yelled Henry.

Lewis leaned over the railing and looked down at Henry.

"I'll haunt you myself," he said.

Henry giggled.

"Feeling spindly?" asked Miss Fitchlow that evening.

Whatever that was, Lewis guessed it was the way he was feeling.

"Cheer up!" said Miss Fitchlow. "The worst is yet to come!" With that, she gave a loud horse laugh. Then she showed Lewis how to do a cartwheel.

After a few moments of cartwheeling, Lewis did feel better. He told Miss Fitchlow all about Delaware's mosquito problems.

"Mercy!" she exclaimed. "I had no idea!"

He felt even better.

To Lewis' surprise, the word "mosquito" turned up in Friday morning's spelling test. He got it right. Better yet, the teacher didn't mention that he had gotten it right.

His plan was to go straight to the park after school. If Mr. Madruga wasn't there, he would go home. He didn't feel like visiting the cave today.

But when he got to the square, he saw Mr. Madruga sitting on his old bench. It was drizzling a little and Mr. Madruga had opened his umbrella.

"Well, well, dear friend. I'm so glad you came," said the old man. "I was afraid you might have forgotten me or thought I had gone away."

"I came every day," said Lewis.

"I thought you would, despite some doubts," said Mr. Madruga. "You are a good friend. Now. Let me tell you the news. My letter—no!—*our* letter astonished Charlie. Even Preciosa was astonished. I put the letter next to his plate, just as I said. Then from my room, I heard much crying and shouting and then a long silence. Then I hear the footsteps, then little taps at the door. I open the door. They are standing there. They don't wish me to go, they say. It would make them too sad if I went back to Barcelona. What could I do? Of course, I said I would stay."

The old man stood up and began to pace back and forth excitedly.

"But now, the big event!" he cried. "Charlie has a friend who has an uncle who is also a shoemaker. I have a job! The old man who worked for the uncle has now gone back to Italy so now the uncle needs a new old man. I am the new old man! Splendid, no?"

"Yes," said Lewis.

"Monday, everything begins," said Mr. Madruga. "I must go home now to shine my shoes and brush my hat and press my suit. I wish to give you a gift for your great help. Take this umbrella which my father gave me. Note the carved handle. It is a Spanish dragon. It is said such dragons used to live in Catalonia. Who knows? Perhaps they once did."

Mr. Madruga held out the umbrella. Lewis took it and then shook Mr. Madruga's hand.

"Thanks," he said.

"Until we meet again," said Mr. Madruga. *"Hasta la vista!"*

*"Adiós,"* said Lewis.

When he got home, he saw that there were two suitcases in the hall. A minute later his mother, his father, and Miss Fitchlow appeared. His mother kissed him and his father squeezed his shoulder.

"Are you all right?" asked his mother.

"All right!" exclaimed Miss Fitchlow. "Why, he is extraordinarily well coordinated, having managed some very difficult Yoga exercises right off. He is also the best-informed person on Delaware mosquitoes I have ever met."

"Well!" said his father.

"Why, Lewis!" said his mother.

Then his father noticed the umbrella which Lewis had furled and was leaning on.

"Where did you get that?" asked his father.

"A friend of mine gave it to me," said Lewis.

"But it's almost twice as big as you are," said his mother.

"I'll get bigger," said Lewis.

"Right!" said Miss Fitchlow.

# The Mysteries of the Cabala

*Isaac Bashevis Singer*

Everyone knew us on Krochmalna Street. My friend Mendel and I walked there every day for hours, my hand on his shoulder, his on mine. We were so preoccupied telling each other stories that we stumbled into baskets of fruits and vegetables belonging to the market women, who shouted after us, "Are you blind or something, you slobs?"

I was ten or so. Mendel was already eleven. I was lean, white-skinned, with a scrawny neck, blue eyes, fiery red hair. My sidelocks were always flying as if in a wind; my gaberdine went unbuttoned, its pockets loaded with storybooks I rented two for a penny. Not only could I read a page of the Talmud by myself, I kept on trying my father's volumes of the Cabala, still without understanding much. On the end pages of these books I would draw, with colored pencils, six winged angels, animals with two heads and with eyes in their tails, demons with horns, snouts, snakes' bodies, calves' feet. In the evening, when I stood on our balcony, I stared up into the star-studded sky and brooded about what there was before the creation of the world. At home everybody said I was growing up to be a crazy philosopher, like that professor in Germany who pondered and philosophized for years, until he arrived at the conclusion that a man should walk with his head down and his feet up.

My friend Mendel was the son of a coal porter. Every few weeks his father brought a huge basket of coal for our stoves, and my mother gave him a kopeck. Mendel was taller than I, dark like a gypsy, his hair so black it had a bluish tinge. He had a short nose, a chin with a split in the middle, and slanting eyes like a Tartar's. He wore a tattered gaberdine and torn boots. His family lived in one room at 13 Krochmalna Street. His mother, blind in one eye, dealt in crockery in a stall behind the markets.

We both had the same passion: inventing stories. We never got tired of listening to each other's tales. That late afternoon in summer, as we passed Yanash's bazaar, Mendel halted. He had a secret to tell me: it was not true his father was a coal porter. That was only a disguise. Actually he was richer than any Rothschild. His family had a palace in the forest, and another castle on the sea, full of gold, silver, and diamonds. I asked Mendel how they had become so rich, and he said, "Swear by your fringed garment you will never tell anyone."

I swore.

"Let's split a straw."

We picked up a straw and, each taking an end, tore it between us as a bond. In Mendel's Tartar eyes a dreamy smile appeared and he opened a mouth of extremely white teeth, just like a gypsy's. He said, "My father is a robber."

A shiver ran down my back. "Who does he rob?"

"He digs tunnels into banks and drags out their gold. He hides in the forest, waiting to ambush merchants. He wears a gun and a sword. He is a sorcerer, too, and he can enter the trunks of trees, even though no one can see any opening."

"So why does he have to be a porter?" I asked.

"So the police won't find out. . . ."

Mendel told me that his father did not operate singlehanded. He was the chief of twelve hundred thieves, whom he sent all over the world to rob people and bring back the booty. Some sailed the seas and attacked ships; others held up caravans in the desert. Mendel said that, besides his mother, his father had twelve concubines, captive princesses. And when he, Mendel, became Bar Mitzvah, he would also become a robber. He would marry a princess from the other side of the River Sambation. She was already waiting for Mendel to come to the palace and wed her. She had golden hair falling to her ankles and wore golden slippers on her feet. To keep her from running away, Mendel's father had bound her to a pillar with a chain.

"Why does she want to run away?" I asked.

"Because she is yearning for her mother."

I knew it was all lies and even realized which storybooks the different parts came from, but his story enchanted me all the same. We were standing near the fish market, where carp, pike, and chub swam in tubs of water. It was Thursday and women were buying fish for the Sabbath. A blind beggar wearing dark glasses, with a cottony gray beard, plucked chords on a mandolin as he sang a heartrending song about the sinking of the *Titanic*. On his shoulder stood a parrot picking at its feathers with its beak. The beggar's wife, young and as agile as a dancer, collected alms in a tambourine. Over the Wola section, the sun was setting, larger than usual, as yellow as gold. Farther out lay a huge, sulphur-yellow cloud blazing like a fiery river upon a bed of glowing coals. It made me think of the River of Fire in Gehenna, where the wicked are punished.

Mendel and I, even though we were best friends, were also silently engaged in a struggle. He was envious of me because my father was a rabbi and because we lived in an apartment with two rooms, a kitchen and a balcony. He was always trying to prove that he was the stronger, cleverer, and more learned one. Now I was trying to invent a story as wonderful as Mendel's, or even more so. Abruptly I said, "I also have a secret I've never told you."

Mendel's Tartar eyes filled with mockery. "What's your secret?"

"Swear you won't tell anyone."

Mendel swore with a false smile and a look that almost seemed to be winking at someone unseen.

I said: "I know the Cabala!"

Mendel's eyes narrowed into slits. "You? How could you know it?"

"My father taught it to me."

"Is it allowed—to teach a boy the Cabala?"

"I'm different from other boys."

"Well . . . ! So what did you learn?"

"I can create pigeons. I can make wine flow from the wall. I can recite a spell and fly up in the air."

"What else?"

"I can take seven-mile steps."

"What else?"

"I can turn invisible. And I can change pebbles into pearls."

Mendel began to twist one of his sidelocks. Just as mine were disheveled, his were twirled tightly like two little horns.

"If that's so, you could have more money than the richest man in the world."

"Yes. True."

"So why haven't you got it?"

"One is not allowed to make use of the Cabala. It's very dangerous. There is one spell that if you utter it the sky turns red like fire, the sea begins to churn, and the waves rise until they touch the clouds. All the animals drown; all the buildings collapse; an abyss opens and the whole world becomes black as midnight."

"How does that spell go?"

"Do you want me to destroy the world?"

"Nnnn . . . no."

"When I'm older, I will get permission from the prophet Elijah to fly to the Holy Land. There I will live in a ruin and bring the Messiah."

Mendel bent his head. He picked up a piece of paper from the sidewalk and began to fold it into a bird. I expected him to ask many more questions, but he remained stubbornly silent. All at once I felt that in my ambition I had overdone it; it was Mendel's fault. He had driven me to try to make myself too great. My own words had frightened me. One is not allowed to play games with the Cabala. Terrible nightmares might invade my sleep. I said, "Mendel, I want to go home."

"Let's go."

We moved toward the gate that led to Mirowski Street, no longer walking with our arms about each other's shoulders, but a little apart. Instead of drawing us closer, our talk had separated us. But why? I suddenly noticed how ragged Mendel's clothes were. The toe of his left boot had opened like a mouth and the nails stuck up like teeth. We came out on Mirowski Street, which was littered with horse dung, straw off farmers' carts, rotten fruit thrown out by the fruit merchants. Between the two city streets stood a building where ice was manufactured. Though it was still day outside, inside the electric lights were burning. Wheels turned rapidly; leather conveyor belts flowed; signals lit up and extinguished themselves. Not a single person was to be seen. Uncanny noises came from in there. Under our feet, through grates, we could see into cellars where tanks full of water were turning to ice. For quite a while Mendel and I stood there gawking; then we moved on. I asked suddenly, "Who feeds her?"

Mendel seemed to wake up. "What are you talking about?"

"I mean the girl with the golden slippers."

"There are maidservants there."

Not far from the second market, I saw two coins, two copper six-groschen pieces that lay side by side as if someone had placed them on the sidewalk. I bent down and picked them up. Mendel, seeing them too, cried out, "Partners!"

I gave him one immediately, though at the same time I thought that if it had been he who had picked them up, he would not have given me one. Mendel looked at the coin from every angle and then he said, "If you can turn pebbles into pearls, what do you want a six-groschen for?"

I would have liked to ask him: And if your father is such a rich robber, what do *you* want a six-groschen for? But something held me back. I was suddenly aware how yellowish his skin was and what high cheekbones he had. Something in that face spoke to me, but what it was saying I couldn't grasp. The lobes of his ears were attached to his cheeks; the wings of his nostrils rose and fell like a horse's. The corners of his mouth curled with envy and his black eyes scorned me. He asked, "What are you going to buy with your money? Candy?"

"I will give it to charity," I answered.

"Here—here's a poor man."

In the middle of the sidewalk, on a board with little wheels, sat half a man; he looked as if he had been sawed across the middle. Both hands gripped pieces of wood padded with cloth, on which he leaned. He wore his cap visor over his eyes, and a torn jacket. On his neck hung a cup to throw alms in. I knew very well what could be bought for six-groschen—colored pencils, storybooks, halvah—but some pride ordered me not to hesitate. Stretching my arm out, I tossed the coin in the cup. The cripple, as if afraid I might change my mind and ask for it back, rolled away so quickly that he almost knocked somebody over.

Mendel's eyebrows came together. "When do you study the Cabala? At night?"

"After midnight."

"So what's going on in heaven?"

I lifted my eyes to the sky and it was red, with black and blue streaks across the middle, as if a storm were coming. Two birds flapped up, screeching, calling each other. The moon had come out. Only a minute ago it had been day. Now night had fallen. The women at the street stands were cleaning up their merchandise. A man with a long stick was walking from one lamppost to the next, lighting the gas flames. I wanted to answer Mendel but couldn't think what to say. I was ashamed of my pretending, as though I were suddenly a grownup. I said, "Mendel, enough of these lies."

"What's the matter, huh?"

"I don't study the Cabala and your father is not a robber."

Mendel stopped. "Why are you so angry? Because you gave your six-groschen to the beggar?"

"I'm not angry. If you have a palace in the forest, you don't carry coals all day long for Haim Leib. And you haven't got a girl with golden slippers. It's all a fairy story."

"So you want to quarrel? Don't think just because your father is a rabbi I'm going to flatter you. Maybe I have lied, but you'll never know the truth."

"What is there to know? You made it all up."

"I'll become a bandit, a real one."

"They will roast you in Gehenna."

"Let them roast me. I'm in love!"

I looked at him, shocked. "You're lying again."

"No, it's the truth. If not, may God strike me dead on the spot."

I knew Mendel would not swear such an oath in vain. I felt cold, as if someone with icy fingers had touched my ribs. "With a girl?"

"What else? With a boy? She lives in our courtyard. We'll get engaged. We'll go to my brother's in America."

"Aren't you ashamed . . . ?"

"Jacob also was in love. He kissed Rachel. It is written in the Bible."

"Girl-chaser!"

And I began to run. Mendel screamed something after me and I even imagined that he was pursuing me. I ran until I reached the Radzymin study house. Near the door Mendel's father was praying, a tall, lean man with a sharp Adam's apple, a bent back, and a face that was coal black, like a chimney sweep's. His loins were girded with a rope. He shook, leaned forward, and beat his chest. I imagined he must be asking God's forgiveness for the blasphemies of his son.

At the east wall stood my father in a velvet gaberdine, wearing a broad-brimmed hat and a white sash about his waist. His head touched the wall as he swayed back and forth. A single candle burned in the menorah. No, I did not yet know the Cabala. But I knew that everything that was happening to me tonight was filled with its mysteries. I felt a deep sadness such as I had never felt before. When my father finished praying, I walked over to him and said, "Papa, I have to talk to you."

At my serious tone, my father looked at me out of his blue eyes. "What's the matter?"

"Papa, I want you to teach me the Cabala."

"So that's it? At your age it is forbidden to study the Cabala. It is written that these mysteries should not be divulged to a man before he is thirty."

"Papa, I want it now."

My father clutched his red beard. "What's your hurry? You can be a decent man without the Cabala."

"Papa, can one destroy the world with a holy spell?"

"The ancient saints could do everything. We can do nothing. Come, let's go home."

We moved toward the gate, where Rebecca, the baker's daughter, stood with baskets full of fresh rolls, bread, bagels warm from the oven. Women were picking over the baked goods and their crusts crackled. My father and I walked out into the street, where the gas lamps cast a yellow glow. Between two chimneys spouting smoke and sparks hung a large, blood-red moon.

"Is it true that people live there?" I asked.

My father was silent for a while. "What makes you think so? Nothing is known. Cabala is only for strong brains.

When weak little brains are immersed in the Cabala—one can easily fall into insanity."

My father's words frightened me. I felt myself close to madness.

He said, "You are still a boy. When, God willing, you grow up, get married, have more sense, then you will find out what you can do."

"I'm not going to get married."

"What else? Stay a bachelor? It is written: 'He created it not in vain. He formed it to be inhabited.' You will grow up, be matched with a girl, and get engaged."

"What girl?"

"Who can know in advance?"

At that moment I realized why I was so sad. The street was full of girls but I didn't know who was going to be my betrothed. She, the one destined for me, didn't know either. It could be that we both bought candy in the same store, that we passed each other, looked at each other, not knowing that we were going to be man and wife. I began to look among the crowd. The street was full of girls my age, some a little younger, some older. One walked and licked an ice-cream cone. Another one nibbled cheesecake at Esther's candy store, holding it between her thumb and middle finger, with her pinky lifted up elegantly. A girl carrying books and notebooks under her arm, with red ribbons in her braids, a pleated skirt, and a black apron, had black-stockinged legs that looked like a doll's. The streets were full of the aroma of fresh bagels, of breezes coming from the Vistula, and the Praga forest. Around the street lamps a myriad of winged creatures—moths, butterflies, gnats—whirled, deceived by the light into believing night was day. I looked at the upper floors, where girls stood on balconies, gazed out of windows. They were talking, singing, laughing. I listened to the noise of sewing machines, to a gramophone playing. Behind a window I saw the dark shadow of a girl. I imagined she was staring at me through the mesh of the curtain. I said to my father, "Papa, can you find out from the Cabala who you are going to get engaged to?"

My father stopped. "What do you have to know for? They know in heaven and that is enough."

For a while we walked in silence. Then my father asked, "Son, what has happened to you?"

All the lampposts became bent and all the lights foggy as my eyes filled with tears. "Papa, I don't know."

"You are growing up, my son. That is what is happening to you."

And my father suddenly did something he had never done before: he bent down and kissed my forehead.

# BAD CHARACTERS

*Jean Stafford*

Up until I learned my lesson in a very bitter way, I never had more than one friend at a time, and my friendships, though ardent, were short. When they ended and I was sent packing in unforgetting indignation, it was always my fault; I would swear vilely in front of a girl I knew to be pious and prim (by the time I was eight, the most grandiloquent gangster could have added nothing to my vocabulary—I had an awful tongue), or I would call a Tenderfoot Scout a sissy or make fun of athletics to the daughter of the high school coach. These outbursts came without plan; I would simply one day, in the middle of a game of Russian bank or a hike or a conversation, be possessed with a passion to be by myself, and my lips instantly and without warning would accommodate me. My friend was never more surprised than I was when this irrevocable slander, this terrible, talented invective, came boiling out of my mouth.

Afterward, when I had got the solitude I had wanted, I was dismayed, for I did not like it. Then I would sadly finish the game of cards as if someone were still across the table from me; I would sit down on the mesa and through a glaze of tears would watch my friend departing with outraged strides; mournfully, I would talk to myself. Because I had already alienated everyone I knew, I then had nowhere to turn, so a famine set in and I would have no companion but Muff, the cat, who loathed all human beings except, significantly, me—truly. She bit and scratched the hands that fed her, she arched her back like a Halloween cat if someone kindly tried to pet her, she hissed, laid her ears flat to her skull, growled, fluffed up her tail into a great bush and flailed it like a bullwhack. But she purred for me, she patted me with her paws, keeping her claws in their velvet scabbards. She was not only an ill-natured cat, she was also badly dressed. She was a calico, and the distribution of her colors was a mess; she looked as if she had been left out in the rain and her paint had run. She had a Roman nose as the result of some early injury, her tail was skinny, she had a perfectly venomous look in her eye. My family said—my family discriminated against me—that I was much closer kin to Muff than I was to any of them. To tease me into a tantrum, my brother Jack and my sister Stella often called me Kitty instead of Emily. Little Tess did not dare, because she knew I'd chloroform her if she did. Jack, the meanest boy I have ever known in my life, called me Polecat and talked about my mania for fish, which, it so happened, I despised. The name would have been far more appropriate for *him,* since he trapped

skunks up in the foothills—we lived in Adams, Colorado—
and quite often, because he was careless and foolhardy, his
clothes had to be buried, and even when that was done, he
sometimes was sent home from school on the complaint
of girls sitting next to him.

Along about Christmastime when I was eleven, I was
making a snowman with Virgil Meade in his backyard, and
all of a sudden, just as we had got around to the right arm,
I had to be alone. So I called him a son of a sea cook, said
it was common knowledge that his mother had bedbugs
and that his father, a dentist and the deputy marshal, was a
bootlegger on the side. For a moment, Virgil was too aghast
to speak—a little earlier we had agreed to marry someday
and become millionaires—and then, with a bellow of fury,
he knocked me down and washed my face in snow. I saw
stars, and black balls bounced before my eyes. When finally
he let me up, we were both crying, and he hollered that if
I didn't get off his property that instant, his father would
arrest me and send me to Canon City. I trudged slowly
home, half frozen, critically sick at heart. So it was old Muff
again for me for quite some time. Old Muff, that is, until I
met Lottie Jump, although "met" is a euphemism for the
way I first encountered her.

I saw Lottie for the first time one afternoon in our own
kitchen, stealing a chocolate cake. Stella and Jack had not
come home from school yet—not having my difficult
disposition, they were popular, and they were at their
friends' houses, pulling taffy, I suppose, making popcorn

balls, playing casino, having fun—and my mother had taken Tess with her to visit a friend in one of the T.B. sanitariums. I was alone in the house, and making a funny-looking Christmas card, although I had no one to send it to. When I heard someone in the kitchen, I thought it was Mother home early, and I went out to ask her why the green pine tree I had pasted on a square of red paper looked as if it were falling down. And there, instead of Mother and my baby sister, was this pale, conspicuous child in the act of lifting the glass cover from the devil's-food my mother had taken out of the oven an hour before and set on the plant shelf by the window. The child had her back to me, and when she heard my footfall, she wheeled with an amazing look of fear and hatred on her pinched and pasty face. Simultaneously, she put the cover over the cake again, and then she stood motionless as if she were under a spell.

I was scared, for I was not sure what was happening, and anyhow it gives you a turn to find a stranger in the kitchen in the middle of the afternoon, even if the stranger is only a skinny child in a moldy coat and sopping wet basketball shoes. Between us there was a lengthy silence, but there was a great deal of noise in the room: the alarm clock ticked smugly; the teakettle simmered patiently on the back of the stove; Muff, cross at having been waked up, thumped her tail against the side of the terrarium in the window where she had been sleeping—contrary to orders—among the geraniums. This went on, it seemed to me, for hours and hours while that tall, sickly girl and I confronted each

91

other. When, after a long time, she did open her mouth, it was to tell a prodigious lie. "I came to see if you'd like to play with me," she said. I think she sighed and stole a sidelong and regretful glance at the cake.

Beggars cannot be choosers, and I had been missing Virgil so sorely, as well as all those other dear friends forever lost to me, that in spite of her flagrance (she had never clapped eyes on me before, she had had no way of knowing there was a creature of my age in the house—she had come in like a hobo to steal my mother's cake), I was flattered and consoled. I asked her name and, learning it, believed my ears no better than my eyes: Lottie Jump. What on earth! What on earth—you surely will agree with me—and yet when I told her mine, Emily Vanderpool, she laughed until she coughed and gasped. "Beg pardon," she said. "Names like them always hit my funny bone. There was this towhead boy in school named Delbert Saxonfield." I saw no connection and I was insulted (what's so funny about Vanderpool, I'd like to know), but Lottie Jump was, technically, my guest and I *was* lonesome, so I asked her, since she had spoken of playing with me, if she knew how to play Andy-I-Over. She said "Naw." It turned out that she did not know how to play any games at all; she couldn't do anything and didn't want to do anything; her only recreation and her only gift was, and always had been, stealing. But this I did not know at the time.

As it happened, it was too cold and snowy to play outdoors that day anyhow, and after I had run through my list of indoor games and Lottie had shaken her head at all of them (when I spoke of Parcheesi, she went "Ugh!"

and pretended to be sick), she suggested that we look through my mother's bureau drawers. This did not strike me as strange at all, for it was one of my favorite things to do, and I led the way to Mother's bedroom without a moment's hesitation. I loved the smell of the lavender she kept in gauze bags among her chamois gloves and linen handkerchiefs and filmy scarves; there was a pink fascinator knitted of something as fine as spider's thread, and it made me go quite soft—I wasn't soft as a rule, I was as hard as nails and I gave my mother a rough time—to think of her wearing it around her head as she waltzed on the ice in the bygone days. We examined stockings, nightgowns, camisoles, strings of beads, and mosaic pins, keepsake buttons from dresses worn on memorial occasions, tortoiseshell combs, and a transformation made from Aunt Joey's hair when she had racily had it bobbed. Lottie admired particularly a blue cloisonné perfume flask with ferns and peacocks on it. "Hey," she said, "this sure is cute. I like thing-daddies like this here." But very abruptly she got bored and said, "Let's talk instead. In the front room." I agreed, a little perplexed this time, because I had been about to show her a remarkable powder box that played *The Blue Danube*. We went into the parlor, where Lottie looked at her image in the pier glass for quite a while and with great absorption, as if she had never seen herself before. Then she moved over to the window seat and knelt on it, looking out at the front walk. She kept her hands in the pockets of her thin, dark red coat; once she took out one of her dirty paws to rub her nose for a minute and I saw a bulge in that pocket, like a bunch of jackstones.

I know now that it wasn't jackstones, it was my mother's perfume flask; I thought at the time her hands were cold and that that was why she kept them put away, for I had noticed that she had no mittens.

Lottie did most of the talking, and while she talked, she never once looked at me but kept her eyes fixed on the approach to our house. She told me that her family had come to Adams a month before from Muskogee, Oklahoma, where her father, before he got tuberculosis, had been a brakeman on the Frisco. Now they lived down by Arapahoe Creek, on the west side of town, in one of the cottages of a wretched settlement made up of people so poor and so sick—for in nearly every ramshackle house someone was coughing himself to death—that each time I went past I blushed with guilt because my shoes were sound and my coat was warm and I was well. I wished that Lottie had not told me where she lived, but she was not aware of any pathos in her family's situation, and, indeed, it was with a certain boastfulness that she told me her mother was the short-order cook at the Comanche Café (she pronounced this word in one syllable), which I knew was the dirtiest, darkest, smelliest place in town, patronized by coal miners who never washed their faces and sometimes had such dangerous fights after drinking dago red that the sheriff had to come. Laughing, Lottie told me that her mother was half Indian, and, laughing even harder, she said that her brother didn't have any brains and had never been to school. She herself was eleven years old, but she was only in the third grade, because teachers had always had it in for her—making her go to the blackboard and all like that when she was tired. She hated school—she went to Ashton, on North Hill, and that was why I had never seen her, for I went to Carlyle Hill—and she especially hated the teacher, Miss Cudahy, who had a head shaped like a pine cone and who had killed several people with her ruler. Lottie loved the movies ("Not them Western ones or the ones with apes in," she said. "Ones about hugging and kissing. I love it when they die in that big old soft bed with the curtains up top, and he comes in and says 'Don't leave me, Marguerite de la Mar' "), and she loved to ride in cars. She loved Mr. Goodbars, and if there was one thing she despised worse than another it was tapioca. ("Pa calls it fish eyes. He calls floating island horse spit. He's a big piece of cheese. I hate him.") She did not like cats (Muff was now sitting on the mantelpiece, glaring like an owl); she kind of liked snakes—except cottonmouths and rattlers—because she found them kind of funny; she had once seen a goat eat a tin can. She said that one of these days she would take me downtown—it was a slowpoke town, she said, a one-horse burg (I had never heard such gaudy, cynical talk and was trying to memorize it all)—if I would get some money for the trolley fare; she hated to walk, and I ought to be proud that she had walked all the way from Arapahoe Creek today for the sole solitary purpose of seeing me.

Seeing our freshly baked dessert in the window was a more likely story, but I did not care, for I was deeply impressed by this bold, sassy girl from Oklahoma and greatly admired the poise with which she aired her prejudices. Lottie Jump was certainly nothing to look at. She was tall and made of skin and bones; she was evilly

ugly, and her clothes were a disgrace, not just ill-fitting
and old and ragged but dirty, unmentionably so; clearly she
did not wash much or brush her teeth, which were notched
like a saw, and small and brown (it crossed my mind that
perhaps she chewed tobacco); her long, lank hair looked as
if it might have nits. But she had personality. She made me
think of one of those self-contained dogs whose home is
where his handout is and who travels alone but, if it suits
him to, will become the leader of a pack. She was aloof,
never looking at me, but amiable in the way she kept
calling me "kid." I liked her enormously, and presently I
told her so.

At this, she turned around and smiled at me. Her
smile was the smile of a jack-o'-lantern—high, wide, and
handsome. When it was over, no trace of it remained.
"Well, that's keen, kid, and I like you, too," she said
in her downright Muskogee accent. She gave me a long,
appraising look. Her eyes were the color of mud. "Listen,
kid, how much do you like me?"

"I like you loads, Lottie," I said. "Better than anybody
else, and I'm not kidding."

"You want to be pals?"

"Do I!" I cried. So *there,* Virgil Meade, you big fat
hootnanny, I thought.

"All right, kid, we'll be pals." And she held out her hand
for me to shake. I had to go and get it, for she did not alter
her position on the window seat. It was a dry, cold hand,
and the grip was severe, with more a feeling of bones in it
than friendliness.

Lottie turned and scanned our path and scanned the sidewalk beyond, and then she said, in a lower voice, "Do you know how to lift?"

"Lift?" I wondered if she meant to lift *her*. I was sure I could do it, since she was so skinny, but I couldn't imagine why she would want me to.

"Shoplift, I mean. Like in the five-and-dime."

I did not know the term, and Lottie scowled at my stupidity.

"*Steal*, for crying in the beer!" she said impatiently. This she said so loudly that Muff jumped down from the mantel and left the room in contempt.

I was thrilled to death and shocked to pieces. "Stealing is a sin," I said. "You get put in jail for it."

"Ish ka bibble! I should worry if it's a sin or not," said Lottie, with a shrug. "And they'll never put a smart old whatsis like *me* in jail. It's fun, stealing is—it's a picnic. I'll teach you if you want to learn, kid." Shamelessly she winked at me and grinned again. (That grin! She could have taken it off her face and put it on the table.) And she added, "If you don't, we can't be pals, because lifting is the only kind of playing I like. I hate those dumb games like Statues. Kick-the-Can—phooey!"

I was torn between agitation (I went to Sunday school and knew already about morality; Judge Bay, a crabby old man who loved to punish sinners, was a friend of my father's and once had given Jack a lecture on the criminal mind when he came to call and found Jack looking up an answer in his arithmetic book) and excitement over the

daring invitation to misconduct myself in so perilous a
way. My life, on reflection, looked deadly prim; all I'd ever
done to vary the monotony of it was to swear. I knew that
Lottie Jump meant what she said—that I could have her
friendship only on her terms (plainly, she had gone it alone
for a long time and could go it alone for the rest of her
life)—and although I trembled like an aspen and my heart
went pit-a-pat, I said, "I want to be pals with you, Lottie."

"All right, Vanderpool," said Lottie, and got off the
window seat. "I wouldn't go braggin' about it if I was you.
I wouldn't go telling my ma and pa and the next-door
neighbor that you and Lottie Jump are going down to the
five-and-dime next Saturday aft and lift us some nice rings
and garters and things like that. I mean it, kid." And she
drew the back of her forefinger across her throat and made
a dire face.

"I won't. I promise I won't. My *gosh*, why would I?"

"That's the ticket," said Lottie, with a grin. "I'll meet you
at the trolley shelter at two o'clock. You have the money.
For both down and up. I ain't going to climb up that
ornery hill after I've had my fun."

"Yes, Lottie," I said. Where was I going to get twenty
cents? I was going to have to start stealing before she even
taught me how. Lottie was facing the center of the room,
but she had eyes in the back of her head, and she whirled
around back to the window; my mother and Tess were
turning in our front path.

"Back way," I whispered, and in a moment Lottie was
gone; the swinging door that usually squeaked did not
make a sound as she vanished through it. I listened and I

never heard the back door open and close. Nor did I hear her, in a split second, lift the glass cover and remove that cake designed to feed six people.

I was restless and snappish between Wednesday afternoon and Saturday. When Mother found the cake was gone, she scolded me for not keeping my ears cocked. She assumed, naturally, that a tramp had taken it, for she knew I hadn't eaten it; I never ate anything if I could help it (except for raw potatoes, which I loved) and had been known as a problem feeder from the beginning of my life. At first it occurred to me to have a tantrum and bring her around to my point of view: my tantrums scared the living daylights out of her because my veins stood out and I turned blue and couldn't get my breath. But I rejected this for a more sensible plan. I said, "It just so happens I didn't hear anything. But if I had, I suppose you wish I had gone out in the kitchen and let the robber cut me up into a million little tiny pieces with his sword. You wouldn't even bury me. You'd just put me on the dump. *I* know who's wanted in this family and who isn't." Tears of sorrow, not of anger, came in powerful tides and I groped blindly to the bedroom I shared with Stella, where I lay on my bed and shook with big, silent *weltschmerzlich* sobs. Mother followed me immediately, and so did Tess, and both of them comforted me and told me how much they loved me. I said they didn't; they said they did. Presently, I got a headache, as I always did when I cried, so I got to have an aspirin and a cold cloth on my head, and when Jack and Stella came home, they had to be quiet. I heard Jack say,

"Emily Vanderpool is the biggest polecat in the U.S.A. Whyn't she go in the kitchen and say, 'Hands up'? He woulda lit out." And Mother said, "Sh-h-h! You don't want your sister to be sick, do you?" Muff, not realizing that Lottie had replaced her, came in and curled up at my thigh, purring lustily; I found myself glad that she had left the room before Lottie Jump made her proposition to me, and in gratitude I stroked her unattractive head.

Other things happened. Mother discovered the loss of her perfume flask and talked about nothing else at meals for two whole days. Luckily, it did not occur to her that it had been stolen—she simply thought she had mislaid it— but her monomania got on my father's nerves and he lashed out at her and at the rest of us. And because I was the cause of it all and my conscience was after me with red-hot pokers, I finally *had* to have a tantrum. I slammed my fork down in the middle of supper on the second day and yelled, "If you don't stop fighting, I'm going to kill myself. Yammer, yammer, nag, nag!" And I put my fingers in my ears and squeezed my eyes tight shut and screamed so the whole county could hear, "Shut *up!*" And then I lost my breath and began to turn blue. Daddy hastily apologized to everyone, and Mother said she was sorry for carrying on so about a trinket that had nothing but sentimental value— she was just vexed with herself for being careless, that was all, and she wasn't going to say another word about it.

I never heard so many references to stealing and cake, and even to Oklahoma (ordinarily no one mentioned Oklahoma once in a month of Sundays) and the ten-cent store as I did throughout those next days. I myself once made a ghastly slip and said something to Stella about "the five-and-dime." "The five-and-*dime*!" she exclaimed. "Where'd you get *that* kind of talk? Do you by any chance have reference to the *ten-cent store*?"

The worst of all was Friday night—the very night before I was to meet Lottie Jump—when Judge Bay came to play two-handed pinochle with Daddy. The Judge, a giant in intimidating haberdashery—for some reason, the white piping on his vest bespoke, for me, handcuffs and prison bars—and with an aura of disapproval for almost everything on earth except what pertained directly to himself, was telling Daddy, before they began their game, about the infamous vandalism that had been going on among the college students. "I have reason to believe that there are girls in this gang as well as boys," he said. "They ransack vacant houses and take everything. In one house on Pleasant Street, up there by the Catholic Church, there wasn't anything to take, so they took the kitchen sink. Wasn't a question of taking everything *but*—they took the kitchen sink."

"What ever would they want with a kitchen sink?" asked my mother.

"Mischief," replied the Judge. "If we ever catch them and if they come within my jurisdiction, I can tell you I will give them no quarter. A thief, in my opinion, is the lowest of the low."

Mother told about the chocolate cake. By now, the fiction was so factual in my mind that each time I thought of it I saw a funny-paper bum in baggy pants held up by rope, a hat with holes through which tufts of hair stuck up,

101

shoes from which his toes protruded, a disreputable stubble on his face; he came up beneath the open window where the devil's-food was cooling and he stole it and hotfooted it for the woods, where his companion was frying a small fish in a beat-up skillet. It never crossed my mind any longer that Lottie Jump had hooked that delicious cake.

Judge Bay was properly impressed. "If you will steal a chocolate cake, if you will steal a kitchen sink, you will steal diamonds and money. The small child who pilfers a penny from his mother's pocketbook has started down a path that may lead him to holding up a bank."

It was a good thing I had no homework that night, for I could not possibly have concentrated. We were all sent to our rooms, because the pinochle players had to have absolute quiet. I spent the evening doing cross-stitch. I was making a bureau runner for a Christmas present; as in the case of the Christmas card, I had no one to give it to, but now I decided to give it to Lottie Jump's mother. Stella was reading *Black Beauty*, crying. It was an interminable evening. Stella went to bed first; I saw to that, because I didn't want her lying there awake listening to me talking in my sleep. Besides, I didn't want her to see me tearing open the cardboard box—the one in the shape of a church, which held my Christmas Sunday-school offering. Over the door of the church was this shaming legend: "My mite for the poor widow." When Stella had begun to grind her teeth in her first deep sleep, I took twenty cents away from the poor widow, whoever she was (the owner of the kitchen sink, no doubt), for the trolley fare, and secreted it and the remaining three pennies in the pocket of my middy.

I wrapped the money well in a handkerchief and buttoned the pocket and hung my skirt over the middy. And then I tore the paper church into bits—the heavens opened and Judge Bay came toward me with a double-barreled shotgun—and hid the bits under a pile of pajamas. I did not sleep one wink. Except that I must have, because of the stupendous nightmares that kept wrenching the flesh off my skeleton and caused me to come close to perishing of thirst; once I fell out of bed and hit my head on Stella's ice skates. I would have waked her up and given her a piece of my mind for leaving them in such a lousy place, but then I remembered: I wanted *no* commotion of any kind.

I couldn't eat breakfast and I couldn't eat lunch. Old Johnny-on-the-spot Jack kept saying, "*Poor* Polecat. Polecat wants her fish for dinner." Mother made an abortive attempt to take my temperature. And when all that hullabaloo subsided, I was nearly in the soup because Mother asked me to mind Tess while she went to the sanitarium to see Mrs. Rogers, who, all of a sudden, was too sick to have anyone but grownups near her. Stella couldn't stay with the baby because she had to go to ballet, and Jack couldn't because he had to go up to the mesa and empty his traps. ("No, they *can't* wait. You want my skins to rot in this hot-one-day-cold-the-next weather?") I was arguing and whining when the telephone rang. Mother went to answer it and came back with a look of great sadness; Mrs. Rogers, she had learned, had had another hemorrhage. So Mother would not be going to the sanitarium after all and I needn't stay with Tess.

By the time I left the house, I was as cross as a bear. I felt awful about the widow's mite and I felt awful for being mean about staying with Tess, for Mrs. Rogers was a kind old lady, in a cozy blue hug-me-tight and an old-fangled boudoir cap, dying here all alone; she was a friend of Grandma's and had lived just down the street from her in Missouri, and all in the world Mrs. Rogers wanted to do was go back home and lie down in her own big bedroom in her own big, high-ceilinged house and have Grandma and other members of the Eastern Star come in from time to time to say hello. But they wouldn't let her go home; they were going to kill or cure her. I could not help feeling that my hardness of heart and evil of intention had had a good deal to do with her new crisis; right at the very same minute I had been saying "Does that old Mrs. Methuselah *always* have to spoil my fun?" the poor wasted thing was probably coughing up her blood and saying to the nurse, "Tell Emily Vanderpool not to mind me, she can run and play."

I had a bad character, I know that, but my badness never gave me half the enjoyment Jack and Stella thought it did. A good deal of the time I wanted to eat lye. I was certainly having no fun now, thinking of Mrs. Rogers and of depriving that poor widow of bread and milk; what if this penniless woman without a husband had a dog to feed, too? Or a baby? And besides, I didn't want to go downtown to steal anything from the ten-cent store; I didn't want to see Lottie Jump again—not really, for I knew in my bones that that girl was trouble with a capital "T." And still, in our short meeting, she had mesmerized me; I would think about her style of talking and the expert way she had made off with the perfume flask and the cake (how had she carried the cake through the streets without being noticed?) and be bowled over, for the part of me that did not love God was a black-hearted villain. And apart from these considerations, I had some sort of idea that if I did not keep my appointment with Lottie Jump, she would somehow get revenge; she had seemed a girl of purpose. So, revolted and fascinated, brave and lily-livered, I plodded along through the snow in my flopping galoshes up toward the Chautauqua, where the trolley stop was. On my way, I passed Virgil Meade's house; there was not just a snowman, there was a whole snow family in the backyard, and Virgil himself was throwing a stick for his dog. I was delighted to see that he was alone.

Lottie, who was sitting on a bench in the shelter eating a Mr. Goodbar, looked the same as she had the other time except that she was wearing an amazing hat. I think I had expected her to have a black handkerchief over the lower part of her face or to be wearing a Jesse James waistcoat. But I had never thought of a hat. It was felt; it was the color of cooked meat; it had some flowers appliquéd on the front of it; it had no brim, but rose straight up to a very considerable height, like a monument. It sat so low on her forehead and it was so tight that it looked, in a way, like part of her.

"How's every little thing, bub?" she said, licking her candy wrapper.

"Fine, Lottie," I said, freshly awed.

105

A silence fell. I drank some water from the drinking fountain, sat down, fastened my galoshes, and unfastened them again.

"My mother's teeth grow the wrong way too," said Lottie, and showed me what she meant: the lower teeth were in front of the upper ones. "That so-called trolley car takes its own sweet time. This town is blah."

To save the honor of my hometown, the trolley came scraping and groaning up the hill just then, its bell clanging with an idiotic frenzy, and ground to a stop. Its broad, proud cowcatcher was filled with dirty snow, in the middle of which rested a tomato can, put there, probably, by somebody who was bored to death and couldn't think of anything else to do—I did a lot of pointless things like that on lonesome Saturday afternoons. It was the custom of this trolley car, a rather mysterious one, to pause at the shelter for five minutes while the conductor, who was either Mr. Jansen or Mr. Peck, depending on whether it was the A.M. run or the P.M., got out and stretched and smoked and spit. Sometimes the passengers got out too, acting like sightseers whose destination was this sturdy stucco gazebo instead of, as it really was, the Piggly Wiggly or the Nelson Dry. You expected them to take snapshots of the drinking fountain or of the Chautauqua meetinghouse up on the hill. And when they all got back in the car, you expected them to exchange intelligent observations on the aborigines and the ruins they had seen.

Today there were no passengers, and as soon as Mr. Peck got out and began staring at the mountains as if he had never seen them before while he made himself a cigarette,

Lottie, in her tall hat (was it something like the Inspector's hat in the Katzenjammer Kids?), got into the car, motioning me to follow. I put our nickels in the empty box and joined her on the very last double seat. It was only then that she mapped out the plan for the afternoon, in a low but still insouciant voice. The hat—she did not apologize for it, she simply referred to it as "my hat"—was to be the repository of whatever we stole. In the future, it would be advisable for me to have one like it. (How? Surely it was unique. The flowers, I saw on closer examination, were tulips, but they were blue, and a very unsettling shade of blue.) I was to engage a clerk on one side of the counter, asking her the price of, let's say, a tube of Daggett & Ramsdell vanishing cream, while Lottie would lift a round comb or a barrette or a hair net or whatever on the other side. Then, at a signal, I would decide against the vanishing cream and would move on to the next counter that she indicated. The signal was interesting; it was to be the raising of her hat from the rear—"like I've got the itch and gotta scratch," she said. I was relieved that I was to have no part in the actual stealing, and I was touched that Lottie, who was going to do all the work, said we would "go halvers" on the take. She asked me if there was anything in particular I wanted—she herself had nothing special in mind and was going to shop around first—and I said I would like some rubber gloves. This request was entirely spontaneous; I had never before in my life thought of rubber gloves in one way or another, but a psychologist—or Judge Bay—might have said that this was most significant and that I was planning at that moment to go on from petty larceny to bigger game, armed with a weapon on which I wished to leave no fingerprints.

On the way downtown, quite a few people got on the trolley, and they all gave us such peculiar looks that I was chickenhearted until I realized it must be Lottie's hat they were looking at. No wonder. I kept looking at it myself out of the corner of my eye; it was like a watermelon standing on end. No, it was like a tremendous test tube. On this trip—a slow one, for the trolley pottered through that part of town in a desultory, neighborly way, even going into areas where no one lived—Lottie told me some of the things she had stolen in Muskogee and here in Adams. They included a white satin prayer book (think of it!), Mr. Goodbars by the thousands (she had probably never paid for a Mr. Goodbar in her life), a dinner ring valued at two dollars, a strawberry emery, several cans of corn, some shoelaces, a set of poker chips, countless pencils, four spark plugs ("Pa had this old car, see, and it was broke, so we took 'er to get fixed; I'll build me a radio with 'em sometime—you know? Listen in on them ear muffs to Tulsa?"), a Boy Scout knife, and a Girl Scout folding cup. She made a regular practice of going through the pockets of the coats in the cloakroom every day at recess, but she had never found anything there worth a red cent and was about to give that up. Once, she had taken a gold pencil from a teacher's desk and had got caught—she was sure that this was one of the reasons she was only in the third grade. Of this unjust experience, she said, "The old hoot owl! If I was drivin' in a car on a lonesome stretch and she was settin' beside me, I'd wait till we got to a pile of gravel and then I'd stop and say, 'Git out, Miss Priss.' She'd git out, all right."

Since Lottie was so frank, I was emboldened at last to ask her what she had done with the cake. She faced me with her grin; this grin, in combination with the hat, gave me a surprise from which I have never recovered. "I ate it up," she said. "I went in your garage and sat on your daddy's old tires and ate it. It was pretty good."

There were two ten-cent stores side by side in our town, Kresge's and Woolworth's, and as we walked down the main street toward them, Lottie played with a yo-yo. Since the street was thronged with Christmas shoppers and farmers in for Saturday, this was no ordinary accomplishment; all in all, Lottie Jump was someone to be reckoned with. I cannot say that I was proud to be seen with her; the fact is that I hoped I would not meet anyone I knew, and I thanked my lucky stars that Jack was up in the hills with his dead skunks, because if he had seen her with that lid and that yo-yo, I would never have heard the last of it. But in another way I *was* proud to be with her; in a smaller hemisphere, in one that included only her and me, I was swaggering—I felt like Somebody, marching along beside this lofty Somebody from Oklahoma who was going to hold up the dime store.

There is nothing like Woolworth's at Christmastime. It smells of peanut brittle and terrible chocolate candy, Djer-Kiss talcum powder and Ben Hur perfume—smells sourly of tinsel and waxily of artificial poinsettias. The crowds are made up largely of children and women, with here and there a deliberative old man; the women are buying ribbons and wrappings and Christmas cards, and the children are buying asbestos pot holders for their mothers and, for their fathers, suede bookmarks with a burnt-in design that says "A good book is a good friend" or "Souvenir from the Garden of the Gods." It is very noisy. The salesgirls are forever ringing their bells and asking the floorwalker to bring them change for a five; babies in go-carts are screaming as parcels fall on their heads; the women, waving rolls of red tissue paper, try to attract the attention of the harried girl behind the counter. ("Miss! All I want is this one batch of the red. Can't I just give you the dime?" And the girl, beside herself, mottled with vexation, cries back, "Has to be rung up, Moddom, that's the rule.") There is pandemonium at the toy counter, where things are being tested by the customers—wound up, set off, tooted, pounded, made to say "Maaaah-Maaaah!" There is very little gaiety in the scene and, in fact, those baffled old men look as if they were walking over their own dead bodies, but there is an atmosphere of carnival, nevertheless, and as soon as Lottie and I entered the doors of Woolworth's golden-and-vermilion bedlam, I grew giddy and hot— not pleasantly so. The feeling, indeed, was distinctly disagreeable, like the beginning of a stomach upset.

Lottie gave me a nudge and said softly, "Go look at the envelopes. I want some rubber bands."

This counter was relatively uncrowded (the seasonal stationery supplies—the Christmas cards and wrapping paper and stickers—were at a separate counter), and I went around to examine some very beautiful letter paper;

it was pale pink and it had a border of roses all around it. The clerk here was a cheerful middle-aged woman wearing an apron, and she was giving all her attention to a seedy old man who could not make up his mind between mucilage and paste. "Take your time, Dad," she said. "Compared to the rest of the girls, I'm on my vacation." The old man, holding a tube in one hand and a bottle in the other, looked at her vaguely and said, "I want it for stamps. Sometimes I write a letter and stamp it and then don't mail it and steam the stamp off. Must have ninety cents' worth of stamps like that." The woman laughed. "I know what you mean," she said. "I get mad and write a letter and then I tear it up." The old man gave her a condescending look and said, "That so? But I don't suppose yours are of a political nature." He bent his gaze again to the choice of adhesives.

This first undertaking was duck soup for Lottie. I did not even have to exchange a word with the woman; I saw Miss Fagin lift up *that hat* and give me the high sign, and we moved away, she down one aisle and I down the other, now and again catching a glimpse of each other through the throngs. We met at the foot of the second counter, where notions were sold.

"Fun, huh?" said Lottie, and I nodded, although I felt wholly dreary. "I want some crochet hooks," she said. "Price the rickrack."

This time the clerk was adding up her receipts and did not even look at me or at a woman who was angrily and in vain trying to buy a paper of pins. Out went Lottie's scrawny hand, up went her domed chimney. In this way for

some time she bagged sitting birds: a tea strainer (there was
no one at all at that counter), a box of Mrs. Carpenter's All
Purpose Nails, the rubber gloves I had said I wanted, and
four packages of mixed seeds. Now you have some idea of
the size of Lottie Jump's hat.

I was nervous, not from being her accomplice but from
being in this crowd on an empty stomach, and I was
getting tired—we had been in the store for at least an
hour—and the whole enterprise seemed pointless. There
wasn't a thing in her hat I wanted—not even the rubber
gloves. But in exact proportion as my spirits descended,
Lottie's rose; clearly she had only been target-practicing
and now she was moving in for the kill.

We met beside the books of paper dolls, for
reconnaissance. "I'm gonna get me a pair of pearl beads,"
said Lottie. "You go fuss with the hairpins, hear?"

Luck, combined with her skill, would have stayed with
Lottie, and her hat would have been a cornucopia by the
end of the afternoon if, at the very moment her hand went
out for the string of beads, that idiosyncrasy of mine had
not struck me full force. I had never known it to come with
so few preliminaries; probably this was so because I was
oppressed by all the masses of bodies poking and pushing
me, and all the open mouths breathing in my face.
Anyhow, right then, at the crucial time, I *had to be alone*.

I stood staring down at the bone hairpins for a moment,
and when the girl behind the counter said, "What kind
does Mother want, hon? What color is Mother's hair?"
I looked past her and across at Lottie and I said, "Your
brother isn't the only one in your family that doesn't have

any brains." The clerk, astonished, turned to look where I was looking and caught Lottie in the act of lifting up her hat to put the pearls inside. She had unwisely chosen a long strand and was having a little trouble; I had the nasty thought that it looked as if her brains were leaking out.

The clerk, not able to deal with this emergency herself, frantically punched her bell and cried, "Floorwalker! Mr. Bellamy! I've caught a thief!"

Momentarily there was a violent hush—then such a clamor as you have never heard. Bells rang, babies howled, crockery crashed to the floor as people stumbled in their rush to the arena.

Mr. Bellamy, nineteen years old but broad of shoulder and jaw, was instantly standing beside Lottie, holding her arm with one hand while with the other he removed her hat to reveal to the overjoyed audience that incredible array of merchandise. Her hair all wild, her face a mask of innocent bewilderment, Lottie Jump, the scurvy thing, pretended to be deaf and dumb. She pointed at the rubber gloves and then she pointed at me, and Mr. Bellamy, able at last to prove his mettle, said "Aha!" and, still holding Lottie, moved around the counter to me and grabbed *my* arm. He gave the hat to the clerk and asked her kindly to accompany him and his red-handed catch to the manager's office.

I don't know where Lottie is now—whether she is on the stage or in jail. If her performance after our arrest meant anything, the first is quite as likely as the second. (I never saw her again, and for all I know she lit out of town that night on a freight train. Or perhaps her whole family decamped as suddenly as they had arrived; ours was a most transient population. You can be sure I made no attempt to find her again, and for months I avoided going anywhere near Arapahoe Creek or North Hill.) She never said a word but kept making signs with her fingers, ad-libbing the whole thing. They tested her hearing by shooting off a popgun right in her ear and she never batted an eyelid.

They called up my father, and he came over from the Safeway on the double. I heard very little of what he said because I was crying so hard, but one thing I did hear him say was "Well young lady, I guess you've seen to it that I'll have to part company with my good friend Judge Bay." I tried to defend myself, but it was useless. The manager, Mr. Bellamy, the clerk, and my father patted Lottie on the shoulder, and the clerk said, "Poor, afflicted child." For being a poor, afflicted child, they gave her a bag of hard candy, and she gave them the most fraudulent smile of gratitude, and slobbered a little, and shuffled out, holding her empty hat in front of her like a beggar-man. I hate Lottie Jump to this day, but I have to hand it to her—she was a genius.

The floorwalker would have liked to see me sentenced to the reform school for life, I am sure, but the manager said that considering this was my first offense, he would let my father attend to my punishment. The old-maid clerk, who looked precisely like Emmy Schmalz, clucked her tongue and shook her head at me. My father hustled me out of the office and out of the store and into the car and home, muttering the entire time; now and again I'd hear the words "morals" and "nowadays."

What's the use of telling the rest? You know what happened. Daddy on second thoughts decided not to hang his head in front of Judge Bay but to make use of his friendship in this time of need, and he took me to see the scary old curmudgeon at his house. All I remember of that long declamation, during which the Judge sat behind his desk never taking his eyes off me, was the warning "I want you to give this a great deal of thought, Miss. I want you to search and seek in the innermost corners of your conscience and root out every bit of badness." Oh, *him!* Why, listen, if I'd rooted out all the badness in me, there wouldn't have been anything left of me. My mother cried for days because she had nurtured an outlaw and was ashamed to show her face at the neighborhood store; my father was silent, and he often looked at me. Stella, who was a prig, said, "And to think you did it at *Christmas*time!" As for Jack—well, Jack a couple of times did not know how close he came to seeing glory when I had a butcher knife in my hand. It was Polecat this and Polecat that until I nearly went off my rocker. Tess, of course, didn't know what was going on, and asked so many questions that finally I told her to go to Helen Hunt Jackson in a savage tone of voice.

Good old Muff.

It is not true that you don't learn by experience. At any rate, I did that time. I began immediately to have two or three friends at a time—to be sure, because of the stigma on me, they were by no means the elite of Carlyle Hill Grade—and never again when that terrible need to be alone arose did I let fly. I would say, instead, "I've got a headache. I'll have to go home and take an aspirin," or "Gosh all hemlocks, I forgot—I've got to go to the dentist."

After the scandal died down, I got into the Campfire Girls. It was through pull, of course, since Stella had been a respected member for two years and my mother was a friend of the leader. But it turned out all right. Even Muff did not miss our periods of companionship, because about that time she grew up and started having literally millions of kittens.

# CHURA AND MARWE

*African folktale*
*as told by Humphrey Harman*

Far to the east there is a great mountain, whose top is lacquered with silver every month of the year. Upon the slopes of this once lived a boy and a girl. He was called Chura and she Marwe and they were slave children, got cheap and kept by a household of the Chagga people to watch crops and herd goats.

Now Chura had a face like a toad's and Marwe was so beautiful that when people saw them together they exclaimed, "Eh! How is it that God could make two so different?"

That, however, was not how Marwe saw it. Chura was her companion and the only one she had. They loved each other dearly, were happy together and only when they were together, for they had little else to be happy about.

One day they were sent to watch a field and keep the monkeys from eating the beans. The place was on the lower slopes of the mountain, a clearing in the forest, and there all day the children sat beating a pot with a stick whenever they heard a monkey chatter thievishly behind the wall of leaves. Hemmed in with tall trees, the field was airless and hot, and by late afternoon they could stand their thirst no longer. They slipped off to where a stream, cold from the snows above, fell noisily down a cliff into a pool. The water there was deep and upon its dark surface one leaf floated in a circle all day.

Here they drank hastily, washed the tiredness from their faces, then ran back to the field. Alas, in the little time they had been away the monkeys had stripped it.

Marwe wept and Chura stared at the plundered bean plants with a bleak face. The folk they worked for were harsh and the children knew they would be beaten. Chura tried to comfort his friend, but there was little of that he could give her and at last, in despair, she ran into the forest. Chura followed, calling for her to stop, and was just in time to see her throw herself into the pool where, at once, she sank from sight.

Chura could not swim and he knew the pool to be deep. He ran round the edge calling, but it was no use. The dark water quietened, the leaf again circled placidly, and Marwe was gone.

Chura went back to the household and told those who owned him of the loss of Marwe and the crop. They followed him to the pool, where nothing was to be seen, and then to the field, where the sight of ruined plants made them angry. They beat Chura, and some days later, grieving for Marwe and tired of ill-treatment, he ran away and the Chagga never saw him again.

Soon another pair of children watched the crops or herded goats, and whether they found life better than Chura and Marwe had is unknown.

When Marwe flung herself into the pool she sank slowly through water which changed from bright light of noon to the deep blue of late evening and finally to the darkness of a night with neither moon nor stars. And there she stepped out into the Underworld, shook water from her hair and wandered, chilled to the heart by the grayness of the place.

Presently she came to a hut on the slope of a hill, with an old woman outside preparing supper for the small children playing on the swept earth at her feet. Beyond the hut, just where the hill curved over and away, was a village that seemed as if it had just been built, for the logs of the stockade were white as if the bark had been stripped from them that day and the thatch of the houses was new-dried and trim.

The old woman asked Marwe where she was going, and Marwe replied timidly that she was a stranger and alone and wanted to go to the village she saw above, to ask for food and perhaps work so that she could live her life.

"It's not yet time to go there," said the woman. "Stay with me and work here. You'll not go hungry or lack a place by the fire if you do so."

So Marwe accepted this offer and lived with the old woman. She cared for the children, fetched water from the stream and weeded a garden. Her new mistress was kind and so life for Marwe went on without hardship.

Only sometimes she pined for the sunlight and bird-song of the world above, for here it was never anything but gray. And always she longed for Chura.

And now let us follow what happened to him.

He drifted from village to village of the Chagga, asking for food and work but, because of his ugliness, no one would take him in. Food they offered hastily and then they told him uneasily to go. It seemed to men and even more to women that such an ill-favored face must have been earned by great evil and could only bring with it worse luck. So, wandering from hamlet to village, gradually inching his way round the mountain, he was fed by unwilling charity or, more often, by what small game he could kill or field he could rob. As the years passed he grew strong and hard but no better looking.

One day he left the forest and the tall grass of the foothills and walked north into the sun-bitten plain. Here the trees were bleached and shrunken, standing wide apart, their thin leaves throwing little shade. Between them the ants built red towers and covered every dead leaf or stick with a crust of dry earth.

A juiceless land where grass was scarce and water more so, and here lived the Masai.

They are a people who greatly love three things: children, cattle, and war. Standing like storks upon one leg, holding spears with blades long as an arm, and shields blazing with color, they guarded their cattle and looked with amused indifference upon the lives of other men.

They found Chura wandering and thirsty, carelessly decided not to kill him, made him a servant. At his ugliness they only laughed.

"What's it to us if you look like a toad?" they shouted. "All men other than Masai are animals anyway. And usually look like them."

So Chura milked cows, mended cattle fences, and made himself useful until one night a lion attacked the calves. Then he took a spear from a hut and went out and killed it.

"Wah!" said the Masai when they came running and found Chura with the great beast dead at his feet. "Alone and without a shield! This is a new light you show yourself in. Well, you weren't born Masai, though plainly some mistake's been made by the gods over that. Somewhere within you there must be a Masai of sorts, otherwise you couldn't have done this. We'll accept you for one."

So they gave him the spear he had borrowed, and a shield whose weight made him stagger. When the lion's skin had been cured they made from it a headdress that framed Chura's face in a circle of long tawny hair and added two feet to his height.

"There, now you look almost human," they said. "Only something must be done about that name of yours. It means *toad* and no Masai could live with it."

"Well then, what am I to be called?" asked Chura.

"Hm. Punda Malia (Donkey)?" suggested one.

"No, no, Kifaru (Rhino)," said another.

"What about Nguruwe (Pig)?" threw in another.

121

"If you can't be civil . . ." began Chura, taking a firm grip on his spear.

"Heh! Keep your temper, Brother. We mean no harm. Now, what can your name be . . . ?"

They called for a pot of beer and spent a happy evening making suggestions and falling about with laughter at their own wit. But finally they pulled themselves together and found for Chura a name which seemed to them far more suitable than the one he had brought with him.

When Marwe had lived for a number of years in the Underworld and grown to be as beautiful a woman as she had been a child, she became homesick. The old woman noticed her sadness and asked what caused it. Marwe hesitated, because she did not want to seem ungrateful for the kindness that had been given to her but, in the end, she said that she pined to go back to her own world. The old woman was not offended.

"Ah," she said, "then it's time you went to the village. In this matter I can't help, but they may."

Next day Marwe climbed the hill and waited at the village gate. When she had sat there for some time a number of old men came out. They were dressed in cotton robes that shone through the gloom about, and they greeted her and asked what she wanted. Marwe replied that she wished to return to the world above.

"Hm," they said. "We'll see, yes, we'll see."

Then one who seemed the most important among them asked, "Child, which would you sooner have, the warm or the cold?"

The question bewildered Marwe. "I don't understand," she replied.

Shadows seemed to cross their faces and their voices grew fainter. "That's nothing to us," they said. "You've heard our question and we can do nothing unless you answer. Which would you prefer, the warm or the cold?"

Marwe understood that this was a test which it must be important for her to consider with care.

"Warmth . . . or cold?" she pondered. "Well, everyone would sooner have warmth than cold because cold is bitter and difficult to endure, while warmth is life itself. Yet surely their riddle can't be as easy as that."

When she had thought again, as deeply as she could, it seemed that if the choice was between what is usually thought to be good and bad, her life pointed the other way.

"For," said she, "Chura was ugly and unwanted, yet he was kind and I loved him. And the Underworld is feared by everyone, yet here I've met greater kindness than I ever knew in the sunlit world above."

And she made up her mind and said, "No matter what others believe, I'll trust my own wisdom and choose the cold."

The old men listened to her answer with faces from which she could read nothing, and they offered her two pots. From the mouth of one rose steam, while the other sent out a chill that struck to the bone of a hand brought near it.

"Choose as you've chosen," they urged her and so, faithful to her own belief, she dipped a hand into the cold pot and brought it out covered to the elbow with richly-made bracelets.

"Don't hesitate to take more," they urged her. "Neither we nor the pots will be offended."

So she reached in her other arm and in turn both her feet, and came out heavy with bangles and anklets, heavy precious things made from copper and gold, ornaments worth more than the tribute of a whole tribe.

The old men smiled and told her that she had chosen well and been wise. And still they loaded her with treasures, necklaces of shell, rings, and eardrops. They brought her a fine kilt worked all over with gold wire and beads that glowed blue as the skies she remembered from the world above.

"Now," they said, "we've one more gift: a piece of advice. When you are back in your own world you'll wish in time to marry and there'll be no shortage of those who'll ask for you. Go softly, don't hasten. Wait for someone with the name of Simba to ask, and choose him."

Then, gathering their robes clear of their feet, the old ones led her to the pool. Gently they urged her in and she rose like a thought until she broke the sunlit surface, where the leaf still circled and birds sang in the trees about.

She left the water, sat upon the bank with the light dancing on her finery, and waited for the world to find her.

And very soon it did.

News spread that beside a pool in the forest sat a woman, rich and of amazing beauty, waiting for a husband. They flocked to her with offers, handsome young men, rich landowners, daring hunters, great warriors, even powerful chiefs. And all singing much the same tune, "Here's fame or wealth or power or glory or beauty or . . . if only you'll marry me!"

She pointed at each one of them the same sharp little question, "What's your name?"

"Name! Why, it's Nyati or Mamba or Tembo or Ndovu or . . ." and so on. No end of names and at all she shook her head and replied, "I'm sorry, but that will not be the name of my husband."

Now the news flew even as far as the plain, down where the cattle trudge through the dust, the lion hunts, and the vulture sits upon the thorn. At last it reached Chura, and at once he took spear and shield and came tirelessly running and his heart singing, "Marwe's back from the Underworld and I'll see her!"

When he came to where she sat beside her pool and cried "Marwe!" she recognized his ugliness even framed as it was by a lion's mane. Part of her laughed and the rest wept.

"Oh, Chura," she cried. "Why is life so unkind? I shall never love anyone but you, yet my fate says that we can't marry."

"Then who can you marry?" he demanded.

"Only a man named Simba."

"But that's my name," he roared. "Simba! Lion! The Masai named me that when I killed a lion."

So, of course, they were married. What was there to stop them? It would have been striking fate across the face not to marry. But everyone marveled that so beautiful a woman should choose so ugly a husband.

They paid no attention to them and—it's a strange thing and scarcely to be believed—but, do you know, the moment they were married something happened to his ugly toad's face and he became good to look at.

Well, passable.

So they say.

I don't imagine for one moment that Marwe cared either way.

# SUPERSTITIONS

*Mary La Chapelle*

Frances slept in her clothes. This was a recent practice she had adopted from Jimmy after finding him one morning under his covers outfitted in his miniature army costume. As he popped out of his covers and swung his weedy legs over the bed, his sister was further puzzled to see his feet still shod in his little army boots.

"Jimmy, they're muddy."

He had looked at his dangling feet and reached down to flick a piece of dirt encrusted in the soles of his boots.

"Why did you wear play clothes to bed?"

"I always do." He hopped off his bed and began tapping his boot against the bedstead, causing the mud to flake off in a pile on the floor.

"Well, I know you didn't always. Why do you want to?"

"Simple, Franny, that way I'm ready to play as soon as I wake up."

Now for the last three days, Frances had slept in her red Buster Brown shirt and her light blue cutoffs. As she meandered into wakefulness, she found a specific comfort in fingering the familiar clothing.

It was an early June morning, a week into the summer vacation. Frances held on to her sleep even as the sun came into her bedroom and lay across her forehead like a warm rag. But when the light became so bright that she needed to cover her eyes with her arm, she woke up and rolled onto one elbow so she could rest her chin on the window ledge by her bed. She blinked her eyes. From two stories up the grass looked wavy like water.

Frances turned from the window and looked around the squareness of her room. Reassured that she had gone nowhere else in the night, she slipped out of her tight covers from the top. This was another time-saving trick Jimmy had taught her. He theorized that little kids who got in from the top and out from the top never had to make their beds. "Just punch the pillow and that is that."

She stood for a moment by the bed and looked out at the day-to-be. In the sky two swallows spiraled erratically downward. They looked more to be falling than flying. Away from the window she turned to face the half-open door.

She closed her eyes and touched her fingers to the wall just above her bedpost, then walked like this, eyes closed, her one hand guiding her along the wall out of her room and down the hall. She was apprehensive as she brushed on toward the attic, because if she were to find it had been left open, it would be a bad sign that she couldn't change. Her hand hesitated at the doorway molding as a draft wafted over the little hairs on her wrist. The door was open. She passed her hand over empty space, making believe there was a door there. This didn't help, and the panic she had dreaded surged up from her stomach, making her run blindly down the hall until she was at the opening of the stairway. She bent over to feel where the first step began and sat down on the landing. Her eyes were still closed, she pressed them against her knees, and the pressure created white lights under her eyelids.

This ritual of the blind walk through the upstairs hall was one Frances had adopted herself. She had not taught it to Jimmy because it made no sense. Just as it made no sense to be afraid of an open attic. It was something she had begun, and now she was compelled to continue.

Frances sat at the top of the stairs with her eyes pressed against her knees. Something bad was going to happen; and there was nothing she could do about it. She was trying not to think about the attic, and she wished she had never made up the rule. She muttered aloud, "I just made it up. It's silly, so nothing can happen."

Frances found no one in the kitchen, but she heard sounds indicating that the others were out of bed. Her father was at work. Her mother was in the sewing room in the basement. She could hear the steady whirr of the machine, and then it stopped, shortly to be replaced by the sound of scissors snipping. The racket of cartoons was coming from the TV room along with Jimmy's shrill giggles. Frances

chose a firm banana from the bunch on the counter and
went to join her brother.

Frances once heard her mother confide to Mrs. Benson
that Jimmy was hyperactive. Her grandmother called him
high-strung. Frances liked to watch his green eyes when
they danced on the wake of one of his ideas. His freckles,
too, they danced. Or it seemed to Frances, at least, that
they moved about on his face, and as long as she needed
to blink she would never be sure.

Jimmy's black hair was controlled by some strange static
that caused it to stand up in little tufts, always, as if he had
just taken off a wool stocking cap. His father would wet it
and comb it, saying, "Kiddo, we are going to train your
hair to stay put." But half an hour later Jimmy's hair would
be sticking up all over again.

Frances believed that Jimmy had more God-given life
than she had. It was the bravery that made the difference.
He had more life to risk than she had, and she stayed close
to him for need of the bravery.

Of the two, Frances thought she was the stronger. She
was tall with the dark skin of her Indian grandmother.
Jimmy was fair, his skin translucent, the veins lying close
to the surface. He was slight and smaller than he should be
for his age. Sometimes she would use this against him and
say, "I'm ten and you're a puny eight-year-old." But that
was only when she felt the least brave in the face of him.
The times she did feel truly stronger, she said nothing.
Sometimes as they sat arm against arm on the sofa, and
he looked ahead distracted by the TV, she would trace
the veins in his fine hand with her finger, and that quiet

tenderness would come over her. She would move closer to him and cover his whole arm with her own, laying her brown hand over his so each of her fingers covered one of his, and nothing was left exposed.

His energy overflowed the confines of his body sometimes, like popcorn popping out of a pot too small. On the day that the Bensons' cat had kittens, Jimmy had come running up the back-porch steps where Frances and her mother sat trimming rhubarb. He stopped, breathless, on the top step, making little hops and shaking in the shoulders. He opened his mouth but could only stutter, "The, the ca . . . c."

Their mother said, "Now, Jimmy, calm down."

He made a short whistling sound through his skinny nose and tried again. "Th . . . th . . . th . . ."

"Jimmy," their mother said crossly. "Stop. Think about what you are trying to say."

Then he did stop, stopped hopping; he stopped shaking, while his eyes ceased to dance and rolled back as though to see what he was trying to say. He fell then, crumpled down like a kite that lost its wind. His tremors began before their mother reached him, and she hesitated as though she was afraid to touch him. Frances looked down from the top step at her brother's closed eyes. She could see violent movement beneath the faint blue skin of his eyelids. In a moment he was calm. When he opened his eyes, they were dull, duller than the time he had been sleeping and Frances had peeled his eyes open to see what was in there.

Jimmy took two different pills now to control his seizures. Their mother kept the bottles stored in a square

Tupperware container up in the kitchen cupboard next to the Kool-Aid packages and the Green Stamps. Twice Frances had climbed on the counter to look at the pills. She took them out of their bottles to touch them, and the second time she almost took one, but she decided against it and put them back.

Jimmy didn't have any more big seizures. But once in a while he had a little one, and he would nod over his dinner plate. He'd snap his head up just in time and then just go on as though nothing had happened. Sometimes his eyes would close while he was watching television, and if Frances saw him, she would wonder how much he had missed. Jimmy himself seemed the least concerned about it.

Their mother worried, and she let Frances know that it was the daughter's job to worry when the mother was not around. So Frances put this worry in the back of her head with all her other worries. Though, after a while, she did not think specifically about his seizures, the fear she felt that first day she had seen him lose himself hovered in her dreams—dreams of reaching for him before he fell into some blackness and out of her dream. Her nightmares were forgotten in the daytime, but she began to feel more irritated with him, concerned about his uncontrollable ways. And he didn't like it when she cared so much, called her "Bossy" and "Miss Big Business Beeswax."

Frances leaned against the TV room doorway. She peeled her banana and watched her brother's back. He sat forward in the rocker, his boots just touching the floor. A large bowl of cereal was perched on his knees. She couldn't see his face, but she knew what he looked like. His eyes were opened wide, absorbed, connected to the action on the television, and his mouth was the part of him eating cereal, eating vigorously. Sometimes he would forget, laugh at the cartoon, and milk would dribble out of the corner of his mouth.

Frances waited for Jimmy to finish with his cereal. Then she placed her banana skin in the wastebasket by the door, crouched over, and crept up behind his rocker. Gently, she took hold of the top of his chair and placed each of her bare feet over the rockers. She leaned back, causing her little brother to slide back in the chair and look up at her. "Gimme a ride, Jimmy."

"Well, Jell-O, Franny. It's about time."

She moved about the room, then stopped to stand a bit in front of the television so he would pay attention to her.

"Is it going to be a TV day?" she challenged.

"No way, Ray!" Jimmy twisted around in his chair so that his head was soon hanging where his feet had been and his skinny feet were poked through the back rungs of the chair. His hands, still holding the cereal bowl, dangled close to the floor. Then he rocked himself just enough to set the bowl down.

"What are we going to do?" She was getting impatient.

"War games," he said.

"What kind?"

"We're going to take an important bridge."

"Jimmy, there is only one bridge, and we already took it."

"Not this one, we didn't."

133

"Where is it?"

Jimmy gave an upside-down smile, grunted; his face was red with little white patches where the veins stood out on his forehead.

"Is it over the river? Jimmy! Stop doing that! You're all purple. Answer me, is it over the river?" She grabbed his arms, pulling him out of the chair onto the floor. He breathed heavily and giggled a bit as his face faded to a more agreeable shade. Frances plopped herself into the rocker and began rocking, giving his bony butt a light kick every time she rocked forward. "For the last time, is it over the river?"

"Don't worry. I'll show you," he said, a smug expression on his face.

"So I suppose that means you are going to be the leader?"

"Yeah," he said, grabbing her ankles and pretending to bite them.

"Jimmy, you were the leader yesterday."

"No, I wasn't. Scotty Tanner was."

"Well, let's both be leaders," she said.

"We can't both be. I'll be the leader before the bridge, and you be the leader after the bridge."

"We need more men," she said, as she fantasized being the leader of a larger group.

"Nope. This is a secret maneuver. We can't have everybody in the neighborhood knowing about it."

"Oh, big deal."

"Hey! You're supposed to obey me now."

"Okay, okay, so let's go," she surrendered, giving him one last kick from the rocker.

This last kick spurred Jimmy, and he blasted up from the floor in one swift movement. He stood in front of Frances, his legs spread with his little knees hyperextended in back. She knew immediately, by looking at him, that he was already playing. He was playing soldier.

He pulled his thumbs through the empty belt loops of his fatigue pants and pressed his other four knuckles into his hips. As he stared her down, Frances resisted. Her eyes started to laugh at him. She wanted to protest and call him silly. But the largest part of her wanted to be drawn into his fantasy, and this turned her expression to expectation. She waited.

Jimmy leaned her chair back. "All right then, we're going to take an important bridge today. It's over the river, like you thought, but it's not a common bridge. I think, mostly, that people don't know about it. So once we take it, it'll be our bridge, and the territory on the other side'll be our territory. Now, I'll get the supplies, and you tell the home office."

Frances went down the basement stairs to her mother's sewing room. Her mother, the home officer, surveyed Frances from across her sewing table and then bowed to her sewing again.

"Frances, when are you going to change your clothes?"

"I don't know."

"Well, I hope you'll know soon."

Her mother concentrated on changing the needle in her machine.

"Mom?"

"Mm, hmm?"

"Jimmy and I are going out to play."

"Where is out?"

"Oh, you know."

"I know that you are to stay away from the banks. Stay up on the trails. Before you go, take this up to Jimmy." She handed Frances an old leather belt of their father's, trimmed down with extra holes poked into it. "Tell him to wear it. I have had enough of droopy drawers and everybody in the neighborhood seeing where his legs begin." Her mother looked over her sewing glasses to make the point, then resumed her work.

Frances held the belt in her hand. But instead of moving away, back to Jimmy, she waited as though her mother might have something more to give her. She leaned against the sewing table.

"Frances, don't jiggle the table. How can I sew a straight line?"

"Mom?"

"Hmm?" Her mother now had pins between her lips.

"Sister Margaret Therase said that God knows all our thoughts the very second that we think them."

"Mm, hmm." Her mother bent her head close to the sewing machine needle and pushed a black thread through the tiny hole.

"Sometimes I have bad thoughts. I don't mean to think them, but, you know, they just come to me, and then, I suppose, he knows. I try to take it back . . ."

"Take what back?" her mother mumbled, with the pins still between her lips.

"The bad thoughts." Frances moved up to her mother and plucked the three pins altogether out of her mouth. "Now, talk to me."

"Well, Frances, if it's important, why don't you start from the beginning and try to make yourself a little more clear?"

Frances sighed, closed one eye, looked at her mother. "Sometimes I have bad thoughts." She announced this sentence, each word stated loudly and with long pauses in between, as though her mother might be hard of hearing or slow-witted. "I don't think them on purpose, and I wish that God would just forget about them so that I won't be in trouble."

"Well, just tell God you're sorry. Go to Saturday confession." Her mother smiled at Frances.

"Nooo," Frances bleated. "Not those kinds of bad thoughts, not sinful or mean ones."

"Are you talking about impure thoughts?"

"Ahh!"

"Well, honey, you're not being very clear then. Can't you give me an example?"

Frances cleared her throat. "Okay, we'll be riding in the car. We're passing underneath the stoplight, and just then the stoplight changes to yellow. Well, the first time that happened to us, I got the bad thought."

"What bad thought?"

"Just that it is bad luck to be under the light when you can't see it change to yellow, and if I ever do that again, something bad will happen."

"Like what will happen, Frances? Would we be in a car accident then?"

Frances pictured in her mind what a car accident might be like. She looked up at the ceiling to see what else the bad thing might be.

"I don't know, Mom. Bad is bad. I just get scared. I think the thought about something not going the right way, and then the next thing I think is, Oh, no, now God knows it, and he is going to make it a rule."

"A rule?"

"Yes, a rule! A rule!" Frances pulled at the bottom of her red knit shirt with her hands and stretched it almost to the bottom of her shorts as she strained to be clear. "I make the rule up first, which isn't so bad, but if God hears it, and you know he always does, he's the one that can make the bad thing happen. Do you see?"

"No."

Frances leaned her elbows on the sewing table and cradled her forehead in her hands. She thought about lying in her bed at night and how the hall light shone in through her door. She couldn't sleep with the light shining in her eyes, but she was afraid to sleep in the dark, too. She remembered when she had first found the solution to the problem. She had gotten up and moved the door to the position of being exactly half-open and half-closed. But as soon as she had done that, a new rule had entered her consciousness. Exactly in the middle, that was what the rule had been after that. From then on she had to remember to keep the door exactly in the middle when she went to bed, or somehow it would be bad luck.

Frances felt her mother touch her elbow, and she heard her say, "Tell me."

She looked up, still holding her chin in her hand and said, "Like for instance, the bedroom door has to be half-open. That's not a bad one though, not as bad as the stoplight one anyway. I suppose the bigger the bad luck, the worse the bad thing that is going to happen. I think little ones hardly count, but I do them just the same to be safe."

"Give me an example of a little one."

"Eating M&M's."

"What about M&M's, for heaven sakes?" her mother asked.

"I have to eat them in order. I lay them all out in rows by color. I eat the M&M's from the longer rows until all the rows are the same length as the shortest row." Frances was finding this a difficult process to explain. "In other words, until there is the same number of each color left. Then I eat one from the red row, one from yellow, one from the brown, never changing the order, until they're all gone."

"Frances, look at me. Those rules you are worried about are just superstitions, like walking under ladders and breaking mirrors. Lord knows why you have to make up your own. Maybe we all do at one time or other."

Frances looked at her mother, and her mother looked back kindly through her sewing glasses. Frances looked down again at Jimmy's belt and felt the sadness of being misunderstood. "Mom?"

"What, dear?" she said as she leaned toward the sewing machine and pushed the blue fabric under the needle.

"I had a bad superstition this morning, and I just can't help feeling that God is going to take me up on it."

"But God is good," her mother said. "Don't worry about that."

Frances heard Jimmy rattling the basement stair railing, sending her signals that he was waiting for her to join him. Their mother heard him too. She raised her head from her work and shouted above to the first floor. "Jimmy! There is no point in sneaking around. I know about your little expedition to the river, and all I can say—and I've told Frances, too—is that you are to stay on the upper trails."

Jimmy made high, whining noises like the sounds of radio frequency and shouted back down the basement, "I can't read you—am experiencing interference."

"Well, you better read me, fella," she called back.

They heard Jimmy shout, "AWOL!"

"When you go up there, tell your brother no more shouting."

Frances didn't answer her. Still leaning on the table, she spent a lot of time sticking each of the pins that she still held into her mother's pincushion.

Her mother glanced up. "You're such a moody bird, Frances." Frances rolled her eyes and walked away from the sewing table with a sort of underhanded wave. It was a wave to half-say goodbye and to half-say get lost. She stomped up the stairs to let her mother know that she was leaving and to let her brother know that she was coming.

Jimmy was sitting on the top step. His legs on the second step were jiggling up and down in his little army boots. Jimmy's body commotion had caused several of the supply items to fall from his lap. Frances said, "Jeez, Jimmy," as she alternately climbed the last few steps and picked up the fallen objects. She picked up one of her high-top tennis shoes. Jimmy had painted it completely black with a Magic Marker so the pair would match his army boots. There was also a little tin compass, which always said North unless someone shook it—then it said Northwest. The last thing was a long, narrow strip of paper that had a representation of the Mississippi River running down it. Jimmy had cut this out of a larger map of the United States in their family atlas. Frances wished that he would throw it away. It was hardly an aid to their minute explorations of the river.

While Frances put her shoes on, Jimmy stood in the back hallway, listing aloud the supplies as he stuck them in his baggy pockets. "Peanut butter and grahams, compass, map, twine, penlight, jackknife, a banana for me, and here is a banana for you."

Frances stood up, took the banana that Jimmy was handing her, and stuck it in the elastic of her shorts. "Here, Mom wants you to wear this," she said, while threading Jimmy's new belt through his belt loops.

"Nice." He hummed a note of pleasure, stuck his banana through his belt and patted it as though it was a pistol. "Ready, Eddy?" Jimmy asked Frances.

"You bet, pet." Frances stretched her brown arms over his little shoulders and walked him backward out of the back screen door.

On the stoop they both leaned down to pick up their walking sticks. Jimmy had smoothed them out by rubbing

141

them against the concrete driveway. That was in the spring, and now the two sticks had become a part of their routine. Frances was fond of her stick; she liked its sanded softness. She thought, as she gripped the stick and walked with Jimmy out of the backyard, that the stick made being outside easier. It was not a superstition. Her stick was useful. She could test the depth of puddles before walking through them, turn night crawlers over on the sidewalk without getting the slime on her fingers. She could knock crab apples out of the trees, and she could knock any wise guy in the neighborhood if need be.

Jimmy cherished his stick as an object of fantasy. Frances couldn't keep up with its many identities: a sword, a staff, a laser gun. When Jimmy wanted to pretend sword fighting with her, she would resist, saying, "I don't want to break my stick."

They walked a short distance along the back fences of the neighboring yards and turned from the alley onto the sidewalk. They headed for the river, which was five straight blocks away. The sun was warm and persistent with promises to shine over everything by noon. Frances stood flat-footed for a moment, pulling up the heat of the sidewalk through her tennis shoes.

Outside, Jimmy forgot himself completely. Frances forgot herself occasionally. She was aware of certain precautions, like not looking into the sun too long.

"Crack, Jimmy, don't step on the crack!"

"Crack smack."

"You'll break somebody's back!"

"Not mine."

"Somebody's. Just play the game. Play it for me."

"Okay, crack shmack, crack smack," and he jumped on every crack he could see.

"Jimmy!" She grabbed him around the waist tightly with her chin between his shoulder blades. He giggled, then stopped. Frances breathed warm breaths through the shirt on his back. He made low growling sounds like a captured lion.

Frances held Jimmy in a grip that said, You can't get away. She might have held him forever, but he slumped down, making himself deadweight in her arms. He hummed a teasing little tune between his teeth. And while Frances became nervous about his tune, he slumped down just far enough to dangle his hands close to the inside of her knees. Then, when he had gained his position, he tickled her relentlessly there. They both fell to the grass boulevard next to the sidewalk and laughed until they ached. When they rolled away from each other onto their backs, she found banana smashed on the front of her shorts and shirt.

Frances scraped the mash disgustedly off of her clothes and wiped it onto the grass with her fingers. She saw that Jimmy's banana had also exploded at the top, and she caught him by the arm, as he rolled toward her, to save him from the mess.

"Watch out for the banana."

"Eyugh!" Jimmy feigned repulsion, and then, making his eyes wicked, he took the banana in his hands like a cake decorator and squeezed it onto her bare leg.

"God! You're such a goon. Why do I ever think we can be friends?"

Flat on her back, Frances draped her arm across her brow and looked at the sky. The sun was indeed getting higher, and she moved her arm over her eyes to block its glare. The weight of her arm against her eyelids brought the white lights back again, and she remembered the morning's early omen. "Let's go to the Connor wading pool instead," she said, without looking at him.

"No, I'm going to the bridge."

The day wasn't going her way, though she wasn't sure what her way would be. She was just feeling hot and listless.

"I don't want to go." She yanked the grass by her sides and looked at the sky again. Jimmy stood up to leave. There was no argument. She turned on her side a little to watch him, and as he walked away, he turned his black, bristly head ever so slightly and spoke the word that controlled her.

"Chicken."

She lay there with her face in the grass, saw a small black ant crawling with quivering effort up one of the narrow blades. After waiting for what she perceived as a stubborn enough amount of time, she stood up and followed him.

On the sidewalk ahead she could barely make out the figure of Jimmy with his stick by his side. She wasn't worried about catching up with him eventually. At least she knew she would along the river bank somewhere. She began to smell the river in the warm air as she walked forward. Her gradual anticipation of its sun-glinted surface took the place, step by step, of her former negative disposition. She forgot temporarily about the cracks in the sidewalk.

The river was the biggest thing Frances knew about. It frustrated her that Jimmy didn't understand how big it was. To him, it was a skinny thing cut out of the atlas, and she believed that he didn't think it had much to do with the rest of the country now that he had cut it out of there and kept it folded up in his pocket. They had argued about its size, but Jimmy still insisted that Lake Minnetonka was much bigger.

Once they crossed University Avenue, it was only a block to the river. As she waited there for traffic to pass, she studied a billboard posted on a building across the street. It was a picture of three men with various kinds of headgear and uniforms. The caption in the lower right-hand corner simply said, "Join the Army." She thought of Jimmy, whom she had lost sight of a few blocks back. Now she wasn't so sure she would catch up with him before he took off on his mission. What if she lost him? She pulled her stick up under her arm and broke into a run. She ran between cars to the other side of the street. Her legs were strong, and the spring in her calves excited the rest of her body.

When Frances came finally to the bluff, she felt small. The cityscape loomed at her from the other side of the river. In the foreground, along the opposite bank, there were many structures of industry—cranes, cables, electrical towers, black skeletal constructions that were menacing to Frances, even in the daytime.

Frances peered over the bluff and called down to the trails, but her voice was lost in the river, and Jimmy didn't answer. She suspected he'd taken the lower trails closest to the water where a bridge might be found. She descended steep stone steps and then made her way along the path beside the water. Next she chose a path that took her higher up to the middle ground. There she stopped and looked around her.

The bluffs overhead were built up with limestone walls to support the mill buildings on top. The numerous tunnels that pierced the upper walls, once used for drainage, were cracked and dry. A pair of pigeons fluttered out of one of these cavelike openings, and their racket startled her. She bent her head back to watch them. The sun behind them glared in her eyes so that her vision was shattered a moment with white specks. "Jimmy!" Where was he? She called again, her voice bouncing off the wall. She thought she heard something, but then it was lost. Then she was sure she had heard it. A small faint, "Hey!" He was above somewhere, but she couldn't see him. She looked higher up to the sound and spotted him. Her stomach jumped when she saw how high he was.

He was balanced against the sky on an old iron girder that stretched out from the mouth of one of the upper caves to the protruding rock of another bluff. The girder looked so narrow that Jimmy appeared to be suspended in air. As she looked at him, the sun blinded her again, and she couldn't bear it.

There wasn't time to take the trail back to the steps, so she began to climb the rocks at the foot of the bluff. Her ears were full of her own breathing, and with each breath she would call out to herself, "That's not a bridge. That's not a bridge. That's not a bridge." The closer she came to Jimmy's position, the more panicky she became, and her refrain turned to, "This is the bad thing. This is the bad thing." But then she caught herself and changed it to, "No, it's not. No, I won't let it be. No, I won't let you do it." She was losing her breath when she finally reached the upper trail. She ran along the upper trail until she was below the cave.

Jimmy was still teetering on the girder. His back was to her, and he was bowed slightly, looking down. She didn't call to him, afraid to startle him. Now she could see how he'd got there. He'd climbed down instead of up. There was even a sort of rock trail coming down from the high ground. A ledge jutted out from the wall in front of the archway of the cave. It was from this ledge that the girder was suspended.

It was necessary for Frances to climb the wall from below. It wasn't far up now, but it took time for her to search out the proper footholds. Normally, she would have been frightened of such a climb, but today she was frightened for Jimmy. Today she was sure the bad luck was his. Once, her footing slipped on a rock, but her hand grips were strong enough to hold her.

When she climbed over the ledge, Jimmy was watching her from his perch.

"Hey, good going, Franny. I've been waiting for you."

Frances gave him no reaction. She could see how rusty and decayed the girder was and understood how easily it could fall apart. She looked only briefly at the drop Jimmy was hanging over. He was above a small ravine full of rocks and other rusted beams that had fallen like this one would. Frances wanted to sound calm when she first spoke. She wanted not to be afraid. She thought perhaps she could change the bad luck if she wasn't afraid.

Her stick still hung from her belt loops. She knew what she should do. "Jimmy, I want you to come back here." She leaned out over the ravine. "I want you to hold on to this stick and cross back over here."

"No way, Ray. The idea is to cross this bridge."

Frances couldn't keep her voice level. "Jimmy, please."

He looked back at her, with challenge in his face. "And I say, Franny!" He began to bounce on the girder singing, "Franny, Franny, Franny." He was teasing. Across the short expanse she could see the dance in his eyes. Then there was a change. A curtain began to close over the dance, and she knew it was starting to happen. Jimmy knew what was happening too. A shred of a second before his eyes went blank, she could see the terrible fear, the kind that she had never, never seen on his face before.

She was on the girder before he began to stumble. When he did begin to lose his balance, she shouted with a deep voice, a voice not her own, "Hold on to the bridge."

Perhaps her words made him respond, or perhaps his own little body responded independently in that dawning moment before the seizure—that time between control and uncontrol. Something forced him to his knees, kept him from toppling over.

Frances straddled the girder and grabbed his belt. She stuck her stick through the belt and used it for a handle as she inched her way backward on the beam. She waited a little as he shuddered, and when he began to come to, she pulled him off the girder onto the ledge.

Groggy, but conscious now, Jimmy cried like a wounded soldier, all anguish and failure in something he didn't understand. He cried like it was a new thing to cry.

She laid her body across his and was quiet.

Jimmy said in small chokes, "I wet it, Franny, I wet my uniform." She felt the dampness too, but she kept herself from crying because she was the older one. She was the one who knew how these things could happen.

She nestled her face next to his and said, "That's okay, Jimmy, we can change it when we get home."

# THE LAST GREAT SNAKE

*Mary Q. Steele*

Bala was sitting by his fireside, carefully polishing his spearhead, when Gatani appeared in the circle of light. Bala stared at him and said nothing.

"I have come for my magic stone," said Gatani at last.

"Have you indeed?" responded Bala. He rubbed sand furiously along the edge of his spearhead.

Gatani was silent. He seemed to be waiting. Bala did not look at him. When Gatani spoke again, his voice was cold with anger. "You have stolen my magic stone. Everyone knows you have stolen it. And now I have come for it."

Bala continued to polish the spear with much energy. When he was done with one side, he turned it over.

"I have not stolen your stone," he answered evenly. "What everyone knows and what is true are not always the same thing. I know nothing of your stone. I have not seen it."

Gatani clenched his fists. His breath hissed between his lips. "The stone was in my house," he whispered. "Now it is gone. Three people saw you leave my house. Three people. Only you could have taken my magic stone."

His eyes blazed above the fire. Then he turned and walked away into the darkness.

Bala went on with his polishing.

In the morning he went to the market, for he had some skins to trade. Anyway he always went to the market on those mornings when he did not hunt. It was a good time to see his friends and hear whatever news there was to hear. He sat down in his usual place, but no one came to ask about his pelts, though Bala and his wife had prepared them carefully.

Bala's wife wished to trade for seeds for her garden and the stuff with which to make a new fish net and perhaps a small metal ornament for her little daughter's neck.

The people in the market did not speak to Bala. Many even turned their heads and would not look at him. He sat a long time and no one came to trade with him.

Then he knew in fact that his honor was gone and everyone truly believed he had stolen Gatani's magic stone.

He gathered up his skins and carried them back to his home and laid them on a shelf. He took two or three tubers and some bread and his spear and his knife and walked away.

He did not speak to anyone and there were few to see him go, for those who were not hunting or gardening were at the market.

Bala did not say goodbye to his wife and his son and daughter. His wife would be working with her plants and her children would be with her. She need not look again upon her husband, a man without honor.

Her father and brothers would help her and soon people would forget. Perhaps someday another man would marry her. It seemed unlikely. Another man would not want the care of Bala's children, the son and daughter of the one who had stolen Gatani's magic stone.

Bala did not walk on the trail, for he did not want to meet anyone. He walked well away from the marked path, among the trees. And he went quietly, so that no one would hear him, so that he might hear others coming toward him in time to shelter himself behind a tree.

He had no wish to look into the face of anyone who supposed that Bala would do such a thing, would steal anything at all, much less Gatani's magic stone. The stone was not really Gatani's. It had come to him from his grandfather, who had been dead for many years.

Who would steal from an old dead man?

Bala walked softly and thought about the magic stone, which had lain in a carved box in Gatani's house ever since the old man died. No one but Gatani and a few of the honored old men of the village had seen it. It was said to be a clear and colorless stone and in its depth one could see true things, what had been and what was to come.

Gatani fed it every week with the blood of certain animals, mixed with fresh spring water. Sometimes he dared to look into its depths and see the truth, what had been and what was to come. He did not do it often. It was a dangerous thing to do, for the truth might crack a heart or make a brain go numb forever.

Bala saw a hare among the bushes and killed it with his spear to eat for supper. He was a good hunter. His family had never lacked for meat or hides. He had no reason to steal, not even a magic stone.

He picked up the hare and looked at it. Yet he had indeed gone into Gatani's house. Gatani's wife had no sense. She had left her fish lying by the door and gone away. Bala had watched and waited for her to come back, and when a crow flew down to eat the catch, Bala had frightened it off and himself taken the fish inside the house and laid them on the hearth.

Three people were passing when he came out and no one thought it strange.

Only the next day, when Gatani opened the carved box to feed the stone and discovered that it was missing, only then had three people come forward and told how Bala had been alone in Gatani's house. Had gone inside when Gatani was away hunting and his wife gone to fetch water to boil her fish.

Bala was angry with these people and yet he knew they had done what they thought was right. To steal was a dreadful thing. And to steal a magic stone was more dreadful still.

A magic stone, a clear and flashing crystal from the head of the giant snake Conokili, a stone which had once caused rain to fall when the forests were almost parched to powder and the gardens yielding nothing.

Bala could remember that terrible year himself, though he had been very young at the time. The stone's rightful owner, Gatani's grandfather, had done that terrifying thing, had dared to go to the stone and ask that it make the rain fall and the thunder roll. But then Gatani's grandfather had been a man of huge courage anyway, for he had killed the giant snake Conokili and taken the stone from its head in the first place.

Bala walked on, deeper and deeper into the forest. When night fell he made a small fire and cooked his supper. And when he had polished his spear carefully, he lay down and went to sleep and over his head passed the silent stars and a dark moon.

But in his house in the village his wife lay awake and heard the cry of owls, for she did not believe that Bala was a man who had stolen a magic crystal.

Nevertheless, she knew that in leaving he had done the only thing he could do, and she spent that night in sorrow for him and for herself and for their children. In the early morning she rose and went a little way into the forest and buried the skins he had left on the shelf.

But she did not forget the spot where they lay, and it was a little as if she had buried Bala there. And sometimes she would come and stand awhile near the place and sometimes she brought her son and daughter with her.

In four days her father came to take them away to live with him in his house. But she would not go.

"I will stay here," she told him.

Her father was a kind man and he saw that she wished to stay in her own house with her memories and her hope that

Bala would someday return there. Yet he was a proud man and knew that if she went on living there alone, everyone in the village would mark it. They would remember Bala and what he had done and that she had been wife to a man who had lost his honor.

So her father went away in some anger, but every week he brought her meat from his hunting and asked if she needed anything.

And time went by.

Day after day Bala walked deeper into the forest, farther and farther away from his home. He endured many hardships. He did not think about his family often, for he had made up his mind not to. He was a man without honor and he had no right to long for his home and his family.

After weeks of journeying, he emerged from the forest and found himself in a long valley of green grasses. In the distance he could see strange formations of dull white rocks. He walked toward the nearest of them and saw with shock that they were not rocks at all. In the grass lay bones, enormous bones, the bones of some animal far bigger than any creature Bala had ever seen. Rib bones taller than himself and teeth bigger than his fist and long, long tusks.

He was filled with fear and thought to leave this valley. But it was a pleasant green place, the grass was soft and deep, rabbits and birds were there in plenty. So he stayed.

And after a while he knew that he had been meant to find this place and live there. For a man without honor is like a bone stripped of its flesh and this should be his home from now on. He would be a bone and live among bones.

There were a few small springs here and there. Rushes grew around them and insects hovered over them. Bala chose the biggest and clearest of these springs and made his fire nearby.

Although it was warm and he had no trouble finding food, he knew that winter would come and with it cold weather and rain or snow. He built a house, using the awesome bones. He made a hut by standing some of the rib bones up and leaning them against each other in a sort of circle. And then he wound grasses and reeds in and out of the bones and plastered the whole thing over with mud and more grass, and he fashioned a door of skins.

He found a rock for the hearth in the middle of the house and there was a hole in the center of the roof, where the rib bones did not quite meet, and out of this hole the smoke from his hearth could drift up into the open sky.

When it was done, it was a good house, and he went inside and kindled a small fire and sat by it and polished his spear and whetted his knife.

But when it came time to sleep, he went outside and lay on the ground, for he did not yet feel easy in his house of bones. Only when the weather grew so cold that he could not sleep comfortably did he begin to spend his nights indoors.

And he waited for whatever would happen next.

When the first snow fell, he rose from his bed and went out his skin door into the world which had changed, since he first came here, from green to brown to white. The huge bones looked lusterless and weatherbeaten and ancient, looming up in the snow. They looked almost tan against the new whiteness.

He wondered what dreadful animals had come here to die and leave their skeletons for him to find. He wondered if anyone else knew of this valley and if other people ever came here.

Almost at once a man appeared, a man older than himself, with a tired, thin face and stringy arms. A hunter with a spear. But the spear was not polished and sharp-edged and shining, like Bala's. It was dull and useless-looking.

The two stood staring at each other, and at last the older man spoke.

"I have come here searching for game," he said. "I see you have come here to live." He nodded at Bala's hut.

Bala was polite. "I did not mean to intrude on land belonging to others," he replied. "I have seen no one except you since I have been here. I will leave if this is a place where I should not have made my dwelling."

The man smiled a little. "This place belongs to no one but the bones of the great creatures which once lived and died here. Many believe that it belongs to their ghosts or to evil witches or bad spirits. I do not know of anyone who wants to live here except yourself. I come here to hunt. I am no longer young and my eyes trouble me. To find meat and skins for my family grows harder and harder. Here there are rabbits at least. And sometimes deer and other things. When I come home empty-handed for many days, then I travel to this place and hunt where few others hunt. I usually kill something."

"Have you no sons to hunt for you?" asked Bala.

The man shook his head. "My wife and my two sons died many years ago, in a plague," he answered. "And then when I was too old, foolishly I married again and my new wife and I have a young daughter, but no sons. My wife is a good and patient woman, she works hard in the garden, she fishes and sometimes she traps birds. But we are in need of skins. And other things."

He hesitated and then went on sadly, "Our village is small. And somehow we do not seem to have many children. Not enough to take care of all of us who are growing old. We try to help each other out. I do what I can."

Bala felt sorry for the other man. And yet he had not lost his honor. He was still part of his village.

But Bala said nothing of his own troubles and why he was here. It was too terrible a thing to say aloud. Not yet.

"We will hunt together, you and I," he said. "I know where we can find deer. I do not need so much meat. I will share whatever we find and you may have the skin. I am not in need of skins."

The other man bowed his head.

"You are kind," he replied. "But I have seen the deer's tracks in the snow. I will hunt alone today. If I have no luck, tomorrow perhaps I can go with you."

Bala saw how it was. This man wanted to hunt for his family by himself. He did not want the company of a stranger, one who lived in this queer valley full of bones and ghosts. He perhaps could sense that Bala was a man who had lost his honor.

The man walked away. The sun came out and most of the snow melted. Bala busied himself at his few tasks. He killed a hare.

In the evening the other man returned, but he had no deer with him. "I lost their tracks when the snow melted," he said. "I searched a long time and I did not find them again."

"Share my supper," said Bala. "It is too much for one and I have no trouble getting hares and rabbits. They are all about."

"Thank you," said the other man.

He came in Bala's house and laid his spear to one side and sat by the hearth. They ate in silence and then once again Bala polished and sharpened his spear. To make talk, he told the man how he had once heard of a town that had been threatened by a great beast.

"Do you suppose it might be such a beast as died here?" Bala asked.

The man considered. "Perhaps," he answered. "I have never heard of one being seen alive. But that is no reason to believe they do not exist. The world is full of wonders no one has ever seen. There are some who say the great snake Ulukini lives in the hills to the north of this valley still. One last giant snake with a magic crystal in its head."

Bala's heart beat fast. Did this man know who he was and that everyone supposed him to be the thief of Gatani's magic stone? But his hands went on polishing and polishing, smoothly and quickly, and did not falter.

"As you say, there are many strange things in the world," he said at last.

He laid down his spear and picked up the other man's. As though in absent-mindedness he polished it too, until it glistened and the edges were sharp and keen. Then he lay down and went to sleep.

The next morning there was more snow. The two hunted together and before noon each had killed a small deer.

"I have meat and skins in plenty," Bala told the other man. "You may take my deer to your family. I would not want to waste so much, and so much would waste if I were to keep it."

Again the man bent his head and did not look at Bala. "I am grateful," he responded. "You are a very kind man."

He said nothing more but kept his eyes on the ground so that Bala might not read there the question he did not speak: Why are you living alone in this strange place of long-dead beasts and ghosts?

He went away, carrying the two deer, and Bala watched him go.

And time went by.

The winter was not very cold or very long, and soon the grass grew up and turned green among the bones and bright flowers blossomed here and there. Bala busied himself as best he could. He grew used to his surroundings and it no longer seemed so curious and uncanny to live in a house made of enormous ribs or to stumble over a vast tusk half-buried in the earth.

Yet it was lonely still and grew no less lonely. And Bala had every day to make his mind turn away from thoughts of his wife and children, of his home and his friends in the market place.

He missed too the tasseled trees of spring and the returning birds, for in this valley there were few trees and only small ones. And the birds were not the soaring singing birds of the forest but mostly ground birds with quiet sad voices and dim colors.

Some days he walked the long distance to the hills toward the north to stand among the big trees and watch their new leaves unfolding and to see the birds, scarlet and blue and green, which flew among the branches. And he would look up and think about the giant snake which lived in the peaks of the mountains, with a magic stone like Gatani's in its head.

And time went by.

And then one morning he woke and stood up and looked about him. Now that the weather was warm he once again slept in the open, unless it rained. Two figures were coming toward him across the green grasses of the valley. He waited, and when they came closer, he saw that it was an old woman and a boy, a boy about fourteen years old.

They did not come to him but stopped some way off. They saw him, he was quite sure, and he wondered why they did not walk closer to look at him and perhaps speak to him, but they did not.

They made a sort of camp and for two days they lived there without appearing to pay him any attention. He was tempted to go to them, to offer them some of the hares and rabbits and birds he killed for food. He did not go. He was

a man without honor and must wait for others to come to
him.

At last the old woman approached his house one
afternoon. She did not speak. She walked about his house
several times, inspecting it carefully. She even lifted the skin
door and peered inside.

Then she went away.

During the next few days she and the boy worked
together and made themselves a similar hut of rib bones
and mud and grass. It was not so good a house as Bala's and
again he bethought himself to go to offer help. Not until he
saw the old woman struggling to carry in a hearthstone did
he travel the distance to their home and take the stone from
her and carry it inside and place it where it should go and
settle it into the earth.

They did not speak, not even when he went outside and
rearranged some of the grasses and mud and reeds in some
places to make the walls more weather-resistant. When he
was done, he stepped back and looked it over, and then the
old woman addressed him.

"I give you thanks," she said. "Your help was needed. I
am old and my grandson is young and we neither of us
have the strength for doing such tasks properly."

"Why did you not ask for my help?" asked Bala. "I am a
grown man and strong and have little to do with my time.
I would have liked helping you make your house."

The old woman fell silent once again. She gazed off into
the west, in the direction from which they had come. Her
hair was long and tangled and her clothes were worn and
tattered and hung in ragged streamers about her knees.

Finally she said, "When we came here, I thought we should be alone. I did not think that someone else would be living here. It is best that my grandson and I have nothing to do with other people. I knew of no other place to go, so we stayed here. But I thought it wisest to act as if we were alone here. To act as if you were some kind of harmless beast living nearby and to treat you thus. When we have been here longer, perhaps I will think of some way we can be neighbors, even friends. But not yet."

"My name is Bala," said Bala. "I can hunt for you. I am a good hunter. I can supply meat and skins for you, at least."

"My grandson is a good hunter too," replied the old woman. "And I can catch birds and lizards and such. We do not lack. We can provide for ourselves."

She turned away and Bala walked back to his house, having been dismissed.

Still every day he watched them and wondered about them and why they were here. Such a woman, an old brave woman—for courage stood in every line of her face—such a woman must be here for some purpose. She had come here not because she must but because she wanted to.

And why had she brought her grandson with her? To provide her with food and skins and shelter? No, such an old woman would prefer taking her chances on dying alone or living on her own resources.

There must be some other reason why the boy was with her.

Bala wondered and wondered, and was glad to have something to wonder about. Was pleased to wake in the mornings and see the two small figures moving about among the great leg bones of long-dead beasts, two other human beings here in this valley with him for whatever mysterious purpose.

He watched the grandson go off with his spear and come back with food. He watched the old woman making a fire and cooking their meals and treating the skins of deer and hare.

They too slept outside, for the weather was warm and pleasant, and Bala supposed the others must feel, as he had done at first, uneasy about sleeping in their house of bones.

When bad weather forced them all to sleep inside, Bala noticed a curious thing. When the old woman emerged after the rain was over, she danced. She stamped and leaped and twisted; her long hair and tattered clothes flew about her like the branches of a storm-tossed tree.

Bala did not like to watch. She danced for some design of her own making, secret and important. He was intruding when he watched. But he could not turn his eyes away and watched until she stopped at last and stood for a long time with bowed head.

With all his heart Bala longed to know her. Still he waited. He dared not be the one to come forward.

And then one day when Bala was stalking a deer, he came face to face with the grandson. The boy must have been hunting the same deer and somehow they had not seen each other, so intent was each on his prey, until they were almost upon one another.

The boy was big, though not yet full grown. He was well made and handsome, and his clothes, unlike his grandmother's, were clean and whole and tidily kept.

Only his eyes bothered Bala, for there was, far in their depths, something sly and more than sly, dangerous and fearsome. Like his grandmother this boy had great courage, but unlike her he did not know the proper way to use it.

Or he did not want perhaps to use it in the proper way.

Now he smiled, but whatever dwelt deep inside him did not go away with the smile. It stayed there still, cold and hard and somehow more fearsome because of the smile.

"We have both lost our quarry," he said, for the deer had bounded away.

"There are more deer," answered Bala. "And hares and rabbits and birds."

The boy nodded indifferently. "We do not need food anyway," he continued. "I hunt because there is little else for me to do. My grandmother can spend her hours sitting in the sun and be happy. But I am young and must move about. Better the company of hares than the company of an old woman who would rather speak to her memories than to me."

Bala was moved to ask the boy to hunt with him. He too longed for companionship and a way to occupy his days.

Yet he recalled the old woman's words. She had spoken the truth, he was sure. It was best that she and this boy not be his friends or even his neighbors for a time.

"My name is Bala," he said at length. "If you need my help, you have only to ask."

The boy smiled again. "I am Medana and my grandmother is called Kotil," he said.

And Bala went away, as though he must hunt further.

After that he sometimes saw the boy raise his arm in greeting in the mornings. The boy and the old woman watched him too, then, and wondered why he was here.

One evening not many days later the old woman came to Bala's campfire.

"I see you keep well," she said. "I am glad." She paused. "I see that you do not want to say why you are here or how long you mean to stay. I do not want to press you. But I have come to tell you why I am here, for I have watched my grandson hail you in the morning, and sooner or later he will find a way to meet you again, when I cannot prevent the meeting. Someday when you travel north to the trees he will follow you. Or he will go before you and wait for you to come to him."

She stopped once more and stared into the fire. Bala could see that she was reluctant to say what she had to say.

"There is something the matter with my grandson. I do not know what it is," she went on. "It is an evil that lives inside his head. He does not do bad things himself. It is rather that he makes others do bad things. He has a way. He knows how to give another person the notion to do what he or she should not do, so that other person must take the blame. I have come here with him, for I know a little magic and I am trying to cure him. If I cannot cure him, at least I will keep him from harming others. That is why I have brought him here. I have made a chain between him and me, a strong chain. He can wander, but he cannot leave me. Still he can reach you. I give you this warning. Whatever your reason for being here, do not let him discover it."

Bala knew then that Kotil herself had learned in some way why he was here. She knew that he was a man who had lost his honor and with it his family and friends.

She knew that he longed to be once more at home with the people he loved, to have life be as it had once been for him. And that he must use all his strength to put those longings from his heart.

And in turn he sensed something about Kotil. He knew why she did her strange dance. She could not spend a night shut up with Medana's evil without running a risk of being defiled by it. Therefore on those mornings she danced away the bad effects of having spent long hours imprisoned with her grandson.

Bala knew that magic dances were very powerful and he had heard often how they could be used to cleanse and purify. He was again ashamed that he had watched her dance, a ritual which she should have been allowed to perform in privacy.

Now he said, "I am grateful for your warning. I will heed it."

She went away and that day Bala did not hunt but sat by his house and pondered.

And in the next few days he kept a diligent watch and often saw Medana following him or waiting for him a long way ahead. Bala no longer walked to the forests at the northern head of the valley, not simply because he was afraid of meeting Medana, but because the year was growing dry and hot. In the woodlands the leaves hung limp upon the trees and the birds seldom sang or even showed themselves.

Hunting became a real task, not something done to pass the time but something done because birds and hares were scarce, and once or twice Bala went supperless to bed.

He hunted now farther and more intensely than he had before, and it was thus that he forgot Kotil's warning and allowed Medana to find him, waiting for rabbits, crouched in the grass; in grass now turned brown and dry, so crisp it crackled underfoot and made hunting even more difficult.

Yet Medana was able to come silently up to him. Bala had observed before that Medana could move as quietly as a shadow.

"I have killed a deer," Medana announced. "We will share it with you, if you like."

Bala hesitated. He was hot and weary and would have liked some of the deer meat. Yet he answered, "No, I will soon have my rabbits. You and your grandmother will need all the meat of your deer for yourselves. I thank you."

"Very well," Medana said. He smiled and gave a small shrug. "You have been talking to my grandmother, I believe, for you have done your best to avoid me. I know. I have seen you turn aside when I came near."

Bala said nothing to this. He could not deny it.

Medana went on. "She has told you that she believes I am an evil person. Now I will tell you something about my grandmother. She speaks the truth, for she has taken a vow that she will never lie. And if you ask her any question, she must tell you the truth if she knows it. It was a very solemn vow."

"Then you are an evil person and she was right to warn me against you," said Bala abruptly.

"So she believes," Medana answered. He smiled again and went away.

By long effort Bala killed two grouse for his supper. He went back to his house and turned over in his mind what Medana had told him.

The next day he determined to go once more to the north forests. Surely he could find a deer there if he climbed high enough into the hills. There would still be much forage under the branches of the great trees and there would still be water in the streams. No doubt many had fled there and Bala would follow.

He set out early and made certain that Medana did not see him go. He kept a careful watch and saw no sign of the boy.

It was a long journey and at its end the shade of the trees was welcome and the long slope of the hills urged him farther and farther in among them, toward the peaks where the giant snake Ulukini lay hidden.

Was it true? Did one last, enormous serpent lie somewhere among those distant ridges?

Bala turned back quickly and, when he had killed his deer, left the forest hurriedly, not glancing back. Medana was waiting for him at the edge of the valley and walked with him.

"I have not killed anything for my grandmother and me to eat today," Medana said. "It is good that we still have some of the meat from the deer."

"Yes," answered Bala. "Though I am ever willing to share with you anything that I have."

"And we with you," murmured Medana.

They walked on and Medana asked, "Have you lived here always?" and Bala answered, "Almost always."

For it was almost so. His life in the village he had put behind him and he did not think of it if he could avoid it.

"Would you not like to go back there, where you came from?" Medana pressed him. "You must be far from where you were born. I am sure it is so. I asked my grandmother and she said it was so. She is old and wise and knows much. And she must always speak the truth."

Bala walked on but at last he said, "This is where I live now."

And he hastened his steps and left Medana behind.

Yet he turned his head once and looked back up at the mountains where the last giant snake lay sleeping in the sun. Perhaps.

And time went by.

The drought was long and hard, and one day the old woman and the boy came with a leather bottle and Kotil requested some water to drink, for their own spring had grown muddy and foul.

Though the spring near Bala's hut no longer bubbled up strongly, the water was still fairly clean and fresh. He filled their bottle and handed it to the old woman. "The rain is not far off," he told her. "I think we will soon have rain."

She shook her head. "No," she told him. "There will be no rain till days have passed more than the fingers of my two hands. We will have to do with what we have, with your help."

Medana gave his grandmother a cunning look. He turned suddenly and stared northward toward the hills. Bala followed his glance.

"There will be water in the hills, high up," Bala said. "Perhaps I could travel there and fetch some back for us."

"It is best not to travel in the hills," answered Kotil sharply. "There are many spirits in the hills and some of them dislike humankind and do not want our presence among them."

She turned away, but Bala took her arm.

"I have heard that one last great snake, Ulukini, one of those who bear a magic crystal in the skull, lives up in the mountains. Is it true?" he asked.

Kotil gave Bala and Medana both a sullen look.

"Yes, it is true," she answered finally. "The last great snake."

She and Medana walked back to their house and Bala watched them go and a plan formed in his mind. Or not a plan, a thought for making a plan. It worried him, and in the nights throbbing with heat he lay awake and stared at the hazy stars and talked with himself as though he were two different people, with different views and feelings and even lives.

The dry weather continued, as Kotil had said it would, and Bala's spring dwindled. At last he arose one morning and walked to Kotil's house.

"My spring will soon be gone," he told her. "It is scarcely more than a trickle. If you will lend me your leather bottles, I will go into the hills and bring back enough water for us to drink until the rains come. Otherwise we may die."

Kotil stared at him strangely, but she brought out her three leather bottles. Bala had not thought to make one for himself, although he dressed his deerskins with as much care and skill as if he was intending to sell them in the market place. His wife, when he had a wife, had made their bottles and he was not sure he possessed the craft and quickness of hand to do it himself.

"Do not go too far," Kotil warned him. "And be very careful. Watch all you do."

"I will be careful," Bala promised.

He took the bottles and set out. He walked quickly though the day was hot and no wind stirred across the valley. When he came to the forest, he went at once to a place where he had, earlier in the year, found a small stream.

The stream was dry now and the moss on the stones had turned black and the ferns had died. He followed the dry bed up and up, and soon there was a little moisture among the rocks. And then a little higher a tiny rill.

He climbed and climbed and at last came to a real brook, and not much farther on to the source of the brook, a spring tumbling out from between two stones.

Bala set his bottles down at that spot. He drank and the water was sweet and cool. And then he went on.

There was no sign that any man had ever been here before, and he left a trail of sorts by which to find his way back quickly—a broken twig, a little pile of pebbles, a knife mark on a tree trunk.

But there was no sign either of the great snake Ulukini and at last he turned back.

He found the bottles and filled them and carried them as carefully as he could down the hillside and out of the forest. Kotil and Medana came to meet him.

"You have been gone a long time," said the old woman.

"Yes," answered Bala. "The spring was far up in the ridges. And I traveled back slowly. I did not want to drop the bottles. As it is, I have not brought back a great deal of water."

"It will suffice," said Kotil. "In two days we will have some rain and then in another two days much rain, more than we will want."

Bala did not look at the old woman, for he knew she would see in his eyes the reason he had been gone so long. She was a very wise woman, and no doubt she would know all he had been thinking during the sleepless nights when he had watched the stars and found himself two people warring one against the other.

"Did you see any signs of the spirits who live among the ridges?" asked Medana. "The ones my grandmother warned you about?"

"I saw nothing," Bala answered honestly.

"Did you see signs of the great serpent?" Medana's voice was mocking.

"I saw nothing," repeated Bala. He picked up one of the bottles and with it returned to his house.

The old woman had predicted rightly. In two days there were showers and then in another two days rain and rain, unending, endless.

And then there was a calamity. The house of Medana and Kotil, not so well built and sturdy as Bala's, collapsed.

Bala saw it happen, saw the bones slowly slide away and topple. He ran at once and pulled the old woman from the wreckage and helped her to her feet. She was not injured, only a little frightened.

Medana was not inside, having gone to look at a trap for hares which he had set some days before. When he returned, he and Bala searched the ruins for the leather bottles and some skins.

"We will have to live together in Bala's house," said Kotil reluctantly. "The rain will end soon and we will rebuild our house."

It was crowded for three people in Bala's small shelter. There was little to eat and no dry wood for a fire. Kotil sang most of the day in a low, sad murmur and Bala thought she must do it to keep Medana's evil at bay, for she could not do her dance.

Bala himself often walked in the pouring rain rather than sit crushed together with the others in the house of bones, listening to the old woman's cracked voice going on and on. Sometimes Medana came with him. They would walk the length of the valley and back, looking for birds and rabbits. They found no great plenty, but enough.

And at last the weather changed and the sun shone once again and a steamy heat rose from the earth.

But before that happened the damage had been done. Two nights before the rain ended, Bala came back to his house with a hare from Medana's trap and enough twigs and grass to build a smoldering fire to cook the hare. Medana was pleased that his snare had succeeded at last and Kotil was glad of the fire, however small. Her bones ached from the damp.

Only Bala was discontent, sorry that Medana and not he had supplied the meal, sorry that he must share his house and the smoky air with this lean old woman and her grandson. Perhaps he had grown overaccustomed to living alone.

That was how the evil slipped in, he knew later. When he had allowed himself to be angry and troubled and fretted by little and foolish things, then even Kotil's songs and charms could not protect him. Medana must have known the moment had come.

"Today when I was out," Medana said suddenly, "the sun broke through the clouds. For just a breath it lit the mountain tops. Tell us, Grandmother, about the spirits there and what would happen to someone who climbed to the places where they stay."

"They are not to be spoken of lightly," she answered and her voice was curt. "And I know little about them, simply that they are there and some are good to humans and some are not, and if one goes among them one must go with care and protect oneself as best one can."

"Then tell us about the giant snake Ulukini and the wonder-working stone in its head," Medana urged in his sly voice.

Kotil sighed, rubbing her knees.

"Everyone knows," she said. "Seven of them were created. Seven giant serpents, each with a marvelous crystal in its head. They came into the world at its very beginning and they were meant to live until the world should end.

Men have killed six of them and now there is only Ulukini left."

"How could they live until the end of the world?" asked Bala. "If men can kill them, cannot other things destroy them?"

"No," she replied. "Only men can find the one vulnerable spot. Only men have the knowledge to kill them and the sharp spear points which can be used against them."

Medana did not look at Kotil. He kept his eyes on Bala, and at last Bala asked, "What is the spot where the spear can enter?"

Kotil gazed into the fire for a long time. And then she said sadly, "Behind the head. Between the third and fourth row of scales. But it is wicked to speak of such things. The last great snake Ulukini is safe upon its mountaintop and should remain so."

She seized Medana by his chin and turned his head so that he must stare into her eyes or drop his lids. "Know this. The blood of the giant snake is poisonous," she cried harshly. "Should anyone thrust his spear into that vital spot, the blood would gush forth and he would die!"

Bala was astonished. How had Gatani's grandfather escaped such a fate? He must have been clever as well as brave. Bala was not clever or brave.

Medana did not turn his eyes from his grandmother's. He stared boldly and smiled his small smile and said softly, "Six of the great snakes have been killed, Grandmother. There must be a way."

And the sun shone at last and the grass grew green once again. Bala lived once again alone in his house. He did not go to help Kotil and Medana rebuild their shelter and they came no more to ask for water from his spring or any other thing. And Bala was lonely once more and without much to occupy his hands or his heart and so he spent long hours looking up into the mountains and wondering. And his thoughts went ever and again to the great serpent Ulukini and the stone in its head.

He reminded himself that he was neither brave nor clever.

The days had begun to shorten. Bala woke one morning before light. He rose and took his spear and his knife and some hides and a little food and set out toward the north, toward the forested ridges. As when he had left his wife and children he had tried not to look behind, so now he tried not to look ahead.

He remembered Kotil's words about the unfriendly spirits in the ridges. He had no weapon against them. He stopped and almost turned back, for his fear was great. And in the end he made himself go forward and thought only about walking, putting one foot in front of the other and walking and walking.

When he came into the forest, he followed the stream, now full and gushing, where he had got water in the dry season. He found beyond it some of the traces he had made for himself at that time. By nightfall he was far above the point he had reached before and lay down and slept where weariness overcame him.

In the morning he was hungry and ate what he had brought with him, for he was afraid of killing any of the birds or animals he saw in the undergrowth. Who knew whether such killing might not anger the spirits around him? Who knew indeed anything about these tall peaks and the dark trees which grew along them or what he might do to offend the invisible beings which lived among them?

He began to climb again, and as the day went on and all he saw seemed not so different from what he had seen in other mountain forests, he made up his mind not to tremble as he had trembled before. Whatever befell him, befell him, and since he could not foresee it, he would try not to fear it but simply wait for it to happen.

And nothing happened.

He climbed up and down the ridges, always going higher when he could. And that evening he killed a hare for his supper and built a fire, and when he had eaten, polished his spear as had always been his custom. If any spirit wished to harm him, it could find him at any time, in daylight or in darkness. And so he slept and no harm came to him.

Once in a while as he journeyed he had a curious sensation of being surrounded by watching eyes. Did these beings know why he had come? And did they know that a terrible fate awaited him? And did they stay their own fury against him because there was no need, since he was destined to die a dreadful death?

He shook away such notions. All woodlands were filled with watching eyes.

For three days he climbed and searched for signs of the great snake Ulukini. Ulukini was there, somewhere, Kotil had said so. But perhaps Bala was not the one meant to discover it. The thought was a happy one. He need not risk death by poison. And yet he went on searching.

And one morning he climbed the highest ridge he had yet come to and looked down into a little saddle in the hills—and there it lay. Ulukini, the last great snake.

He almost cried out in amazement. He had not known it would be so gigantic, lying coiled in a pile taller than a man. Its body was thicker than the bodies of two men and its head was vast.

What he had not known either was that Ulukini was so beautiful. In the morning sun its scales glittered, gold and green and shining blue and purple. The colors moved in waves, the patterns rippled along its back and sides, glowing here, dimming there, but always alive with a cold and vivid fire. Bala caught his breath in his throat. He had not dreamed of such a sight.

For a long time he stared down in wonder. And then he remembered. He had not come to admire. He had come to make a plan and try to carry it out.

He surveyed the snake and its surroundings carefully. This must be where the monster lived and slept. The ground was worn and bare of vegetation—no trees, no brush, no grass. Several wide paths led away from the spot and into the forest. When Ulukini went in search of food or water—and Bala did not know whether it required food or water, being so nearly immortal—no doubt it followed one of these paths.

In a space he discovered this was true, for the great snake roused itself, weaving its huge head back and forth, unwreathing itself from its heap of gleaming coils, and then sliding lithely off among the trees along one of the paths.

Whether it went for food or drink Bala could not know.

For two days Bala watched the giant snake. He learned about the times of its comings and goings, and that it did not see well but used other senses to guide it, touch and smell and hearing.

Bala went away, for he had made a plan and now must try to carry it out. He killed two animals he did not generally kill, for their flesh was not flavorful, but they were very fat. He scraped the fat carefully into one of the hides he had brought with him, and then he sought something else.

He was fortunate and found it almost at once, quartz stone, that rock which is composed of shining crystals.

He pounded up the rock and added the bright particles to the fat and stirred them together well. He made a sort of bag of the hide and tied the mouth tightly with tough grasses.

Then he returned to Ulukini's lair. He concentrated on each step of his plan and tried to carry it out carefully and not let himself consider failing. Or at any rate not let himself care whether he failed.

One of the great snake's trails sloped away to the west. Bala waited until Ulukini had disappeared along another of its paths, and then he went a short way down the western slope. Using his knife and his hands, he dug a deep and narrow trench. He spent a long time at this task, and when he heard Ulukini returning, the day was nearly over.

Bala went swiftly away and hid himself among the trees and in the darkness polished and sharpened his spear and his knife.

He lay down but he could not sleep. He was afraid to sleep. He was afraid to think lest he think of failing and what would happen to him. He lay and looked up at the forest roof above him and tried to think of nothing at all, and then he fell asleep.

He woke and jumped to his feet, believing he had missed his opportunity. But it was still midnight-dark and he had not slept long.

He spent the time till dawn in misery, turning his mind this way and that, away from the happy past and the strange present and the unknown and foreboding future.

And then the night began to dissolve slowly, trees and bushes became shadows and the spaces between them something lighter than shadow. He let himself think of his plan, going over and over it until he was sure of just what he meant to do and how to do it.

When the light grew strong enough so that he could see plainly, he undid his flask full of fat and quartz and rubbed it carefully over his body. He stood under the trees nearly naked and glistening even in the twilight.

He took his spear and his knife and went softly, softly up the western trail. When he came to the narrow trench he had dug the day before, he stopped. The sun was coming up but was not yet high enough to shine upon him. He waited quietly, taking small, shallow breaths.

He could see above him the shadow of Ulukini coiled asleep at the top of the rise. And then the sun climbed a little higher in the sky and the time had come. The rays fell upon him and he shone like a burning tree. Ulukini would be dazzled, its half-blind eyes would never find this glaring object in the glaring light of daybreak.

Bala shouted, "Ulukini! Oh, giant snake, come here!" He called as loudly as he could and saw the serpent's head raised and the long forked tongue come darting out of the great mouth.

"Come here!" cried Bala. He danced back and forth behind the trench, a brilliant firefly of a man in the red and brilliant light of dawn.

The serpent appeared at the top of the slope, hissing in anger, and the long beautiful body flowed toward him, and Bala's heart beat fast. And still he danced and called.

And when the huge beast was almost upon him, its head almost over the trench, he sprang forward and with all his strength plunged his spear behind the head, between the third and fourth row of scales. In one gesture he freed his weapon and leaped back. He ran far down the slope and stopped and looked up.

He heard the beast utter a long, whispering groan, saw it writhe and slash feebly through the air and then go still.

Was it over then? So quickly and simply? He had truly killed Ulukini, the last great snake? He went slowly back the way he had come and saw that the snake was in fact dying.

The great body quivered faintly and blood gushed from its mouth and from the wound and poured into the trench Bala had dug. The blood smoked and hissed, he could hear it burning down and down into the earth, harmlessly vanishing into the dark depths and rocks.

And while he watched a dreadful thing happened. The colors dimmed along Ulukini's scales, the iridescence faded and went out like the embers of a smoldering fire. The snake was gray and dull and then the body itself began to dwindle and collapse, as a burnt log collapses into ashes.

Within a few minutes nothing remained of the giant snake Ulukini and its marvelous beauty but a twisted ridge of dust. Even the vast head had shrunk and the eyes fallen in and the skull crumbled. Bala could see the shape of the magic stone revealed in the top of the skull.

He could not move. He could only stand and stare. He had thought to do a brave and clever thing and he had merely done a deed full of horror that nothing could undo. Ulukini the last great snake had gone to earth and never again would sunlight or moonlight glisten on those cold rainbow scales. Of all that wonder and loveliness there was now simply this small heap of grime.

After a long while Bala roused himself. He went close to the snake and gazed at the shape of the magic crystal embedded in what was left of the skull. The stone was his by right and yet for a long time he could not make himself reach down and claim it.

Let Ulukini keep it. He would have left it save that he knew someone else would surely find it and he would have done this deed in vain. He took his knife and slid it around the stone—and one tiny last drop of blood flew out and fell upon his forearm.

He was protected by the layer of fat, yet the venom burned into his arm. Frightened, he picked up a handful of dirt and grass and rubbed and rubbed at the spot, but the burning went on.

He was to die then. He had truly killed the snake to no purpose, for now the snake was killing him. He squatted and waited to die, here in this far place by the ruins of mystery and legend.

But he did not die. The burning stopped, and when he looked at his arm, the blood was gone. Only in its place a tiny replica of Ulukini clung to his skin, an infinitesimal snake of green and silver and blue and purple, no bigger than a moth's antenna.

So he would not die, only bear forever the mark of what he had done. He went on with the work he had started and lifted the stone from the skull.

He scarcely dared look at it but carried it away at once into the forest and wrapped it gently in moss and leaves. Then he went back to his sleeping place of the night before and gathered up his few belongings and set out for the valley.

He hurried, for now summer was truly gone and the leaves above his head were beginning to turn color. He had no wish to spend another winter in his house of bones.

He had not left a trail for himself as he had traveled to find Ulukini, but like all good hunters he knew where he was going and how to get there. So it did not take many days before he found himself on the last far slopes of the northern mountains and saw the drying grasses of the valley and the strange bones and then at last his house.

Smoke rose from the hole in the roof and he knew Kotil and Medana had taken over his shelter and he was glad. It was a sign that he should not linger here but travel on at once.

Kotil had sensed his coming and they stood waiting for him.

"We took your house," said Kotil when she had greeted him. "Our second shelter was even weaker than our first and fell of its own weight. We did not know that you would be returning. We are grateful for the use of this one. I will see that it is properly cleansed for you."

Bala shook his head. "It is no matter. The house is yours now. I do not intend to stay here again," he told her.

Kotil looked at him sharply and sadly. "You have done it then?" she asked in a quiet voice.

Bala did not meet her eyes. "I do not know what you mean," he said. He was ashamed of his pretense. Stealthily he touched the little image of the snake on his arm.

"And now you can return," Kotil made a statement rather than a question of the words.

"And now I can return," Bala responded. The three of them stood in silence. Bala thought back over it all, the arrival of the two strangers and Kotil's warning about Medana.

"There is this, Kotil," Bala said at last. "It was not Medana's doing only. The notion was there in my mind all along. Medana merely helped me find it. He could not make me do a thing I knew already I was going to do. It was I who lacked the strength to resist."

"A notion in the mind is one thing," the old woman answered sharply. "Learning how to do a thing and doing it are other things entirely. I should not have stayed here with Medana. But I believed I could protect you."

And Bala remembered how Medana had mocked him and challenged him until Bala could not resist asking Kotil to affirm that Ulukini dwelt in the hills and to tell how it might be killed. He remembered the evening when he and Kotil and Medana had sat around the fire in his house and he, Bala, had been angry and resentful and had let Medana slip into his head the determination to listen to only one of those two people arguing in his mind, the determination to seek out and kill Ulukini.

If he had been strong enough . . . if Kotil had taken Medana away . . . if Bala had gone away himself . . .

"I could not protect you," Kotil said sorrowfully. "It may be that I cannot protect anyone from Medana, but only keep him here, away from everyone, where he can do no further harm."

But Kotil was an old woman. The chain that bound Medana to her would grow weaker. Soon enough he would go back into the world of other people.

Bala looked once again into Medana's eyes. Only death would extinguish the little cold slippery thing that lived in their depths. But because of his nature death would come for Medana sooner than for other young men. What harm he would do he had better do quickly. Soon he would be the victim of his own mischief. He would meet an evil stronger than his own and it would turn on him and kill him.

Bala said nothing of his thoughts. Instead he bade them goodbye and wished them well and began the long walk to his home.

And time went by.

The journey back took much more time than it had taken Bala to reach the valley of strange bones. The weather turned cold and there was often rain or even snow. And Bala had now in his keeping a magic crystal, so he traveled always away from paths and trails. He did not know whom he might meet who could discern the stone's presence and try to take it away from him.

And he went with care in order not to offend the stone and gave it frequently water from the clearest springs he could find and sometimes a drop or two of deer's blood. He did not know how properly such things were done, but he did them as well as he could and asked the stone over and over to forgive him for his clumsiness and ignorance.

In its nest of moss and leaves the stone continued to glow and flash and he assumed that it was pleased.

It was good that he had the stone to tend, for the slowness of his journey pricked him and made him impatient, and he could not keep himself from thinking of his wife and children and the chance that he might once more be with them. Only the care of the stone kept his mind from such thoughts.

And at last he was among hills and streams he recognized and he went more swiftly, though still keeping himself hidden. And on the day he reached his village it was almost dark and he waited, sleepless, till morning before he entered the town.

He waited till the day was well begun and most of the people gathered in the market place. He walked then openly and firmly into their midst. He went straight to Gatani and put into the other man's hands the moss within which lay the shining crystal.

"I have brought you a magic stone," said Bala. "To replace the one you have lost."

Gatani stared at Bala and then looked down into his hands. Carefully, with his thumb, he brushed away the moss until the stone glowed forth. Gatani sprang to his feet.

"So!" he cried scornfully. "You have grown weary of exile and have returned my magic stone to me! You have brought back my magic stone!"

Bala could not speak. That he should have done and endured all that he had done and endured and have it come to this: That Gatani should still accuse him of theft and dishonor.

He staggered as if from a blow and from shock he could not speak. He heard sounds of disapproval from those around him and saw their hostile looks, but in a kind of daze.

He raised his hand and caught Gatani's arm and steadied himself and found his voice.

"This is not your stone!" he shouted and heard how fierce, how hoarse with fury was the sound of his own words. "To get this stone I killed the last great serpent, Ulukini. I give it to you freely, to replace your stone. But it was I who killed the snake and I who bear the mark of its death."

He extended his forearm and pointed to the tiny snake there.

Gatani leaned forward. "I see no mark," he said at last. And he called for two elders of the village, who served as priests, to come forward and look.

"We see no mark," they repeated. "Besides it is not possible that the last great serpent is dead."

Bala touched the little snake wonderingly. Was it true? Could no one see the brand except himself? He should not have concealed it from Kotil. She perhaps might have seen it or told him why it would be hidden from others.

And now he stood among those who had once been his friends, and considered that he had done a dreadful thing for no reason at all. He was not to regain the love of his family or the respect of his townsmen.

He raised his eyes to Gatani's.

"Ask the stone," he said furiously. "I dare you to ask the stone itself whether I robbed you of your magic crystal and whether this is it."

Gatani frowned. He was afraid of the stone and of asking it questions. Yet he could not refuse what Bala asked and he knew it.

"It will take two days," he said after a while.

"I have been gone nearly two years," Bala replied. "I can wait another two days."

"Very well," agreed Gatani. He went away carrying the stone and the elders went with him to see that all was done properly.

Bala's wife came to his side and put her hand on his arm and he went with her to their house. And for those two days she did not leave him to work in her garden or go to the market place.

They said little to each other of the nearly two years which were gone and could not be recalled, for there was little to say. Bala's children had grown so that he scarcely recognized them and they did not remember him. Yet he saw no way to change things and spoke to them as a father would and held them in his arms.

Bala's wife said she saw the tiny snake on his forearm, but when he asked her to touch it, she put her finger on the wrong spot and he knew she had lied to comfort him, because she loved him.

And the two days came to an end. Gatani came into the market place with the elders and stood before all the people.

In two days Gatani had grown old, for it is a trying and dangerous thing to look into the depths of a magic crystal and see the truth. The truth may crack a heart.

Gatani spoke and everyone listened with care.

"This magic stone is not my magic stone," he said. "Bala did not steal my stone. My stone grew angry with me, so angry that it swallowed itself. I do not know how I offended it. Perhaps I gave it too much deer's blood or too little. Or perhaps there was something I should have done and failed to do without knowing. Whatever happened, Bala did not take my stone and I accused him wrongly. This is the magic crystal from the head of the last giant snake, Ulukini."

A man called out, "Ah, you are not worthy to own the stone and look into its depths!"

And many people nodded and looked coldly at Gatani. And Bala stepped up beside him and motioned that he had something to say and everyone listened.

"Once I was a man of honor and I lived in this village," he said. "I have been away for nearly two years. Now I am come home and am once again a man of honor. I did not come home in order that another man should go away and take my place in loneliness and disgrace. Gatani was in error, but he acted as he thought he must. He did not then know the truth. I have brought him another stone. It is his and he must decide whether it shall take the place of the one given him by his grandfather."

"This is so," said one of the elders. "What Bala has said is right and as it should be."

And Gatani took his place again in the market and was treated as he had always been. But everyone saw that Gatani had changed. For though he knew he would never be an elder or a great hunter or storyteller or maker of spears, yet he had always walked with pride because his grandfather had chosen him to receive the magic stone. Now he walked with bent head and seldom spoke and was older than his years.

And what became of the stone from the head of Ulukini no one knew except the elders, and they did not say.

So once more Bala lived in his house with his wife and his children and he spoke to them as a husband and father would. He taught his children songs and games and told them what was right to do. He hunted for meat and skins. His wife worked in her garden and helped Bala prepare the skins for sale in the market. Bala traded in the market and everyone came to trade with him and tell him where the hunting was good and who had a new baby and that a wolf had been seen near the town, and news of such sort.

And Bala was again a man of honor and happy to be once more at home with his family and friends.

Yet sometimes he went into the forest and sat alone and touched the tiny snake on his arm, that only he could see. He thought about honor and what it was and what it was worth. He thought of Kotil and Medana, and of Gatani.

But most of all he thought about Ulukini, the last great snake, and of its beauty and how its colors had once glistened in the sun and now would glisten no more.

And time went by.

# GASTON

*William Saroyan*

They were to eat peaches, as planned, after her nap, and now she sat across from the man who would have been a total stranger except that he was in fact her father. They had been together again (although she couldn't quite remember when they had been together before) for almost a hundred years now, or was it only since day before yesterday? Anyhow, they were together again, and he was kind of funny. First, he had the biggest mustache she had ever seen, although to her it was not a mustache at all; it was a lot of red and brown hair under his nose and around the ends of his mouth. Second, he wore a blue-and-white striped jersey instead of a shirt and tie, and no coat. His arms were covered with the same hair, only it was a little lighter and thinner. He wore blue slacks, but no shoes and socks. He was barefoot, and so was she, of course.

He was at home. She was with him in his home in Paris, if you could call it a home. He was very old, especially for a young man—thirty-six, he had told her; and she was six, just up from sleep on a very hot afternoon in August.

That morning, on a little walk in the neighborhood, she had seen peaches in a box outside a small store and she had stopped to look at them, so he had bought a kilo.

Now the peaches were on a large plate on the card table at which they sat. There were seven of them, but one of them was flawed. It looked as good as the others, almost the size of a tennis ball, nice red fading to light green, but where the stem had been there was now a break that went straight down into the heart of the seed.

He placed the biggest and best-looking peach on the small plate in front of the girl and then took the flawed peach and began to remove the skin. When he had half the skin off the peach he ate that side, neither of them talking, both of them just being there, and not being excited or anything—no plans, that is.

The man held the half-eaten peach and looked down into the cavity, into the open seed. The girl looked, too.

While they were looking, two feelers poked out from the cavity. They were attached to a kind of brown knob-head, which followed the feelers, and then two large legs took a strong grip on the edge of the cavity and hoisted some of the rest of whatever it was out of the seed, and stopped there a moment, as if to look around.

The man studied the seed dweller, and so, of course, did the girl.

The creature paused only a fraction of a second, and then continued to come out of the seed, to walk down the eaten side of the peach to wherever it was going.

The girl had never seen anything like it—a whole big thing made out of brown color, a knob-head, feelers, and a great many legs. It was very active, too. Almost businesslike, you might say. The man placed the peach back on the plate. The creature moved off the peach onto the surface of the white plate. There it came to a thoughtful stop.

"Who is it?" the girl said.

"Gaston."

"Where does he live?"

"Well, he used to live in this peach seed, but now that the peach has been harvested and sold, and I have eaten half of it, it looks as if he's out of house and home."

"Aren't you going to squash him?"

"No, of course not, why should I?"

"He's a bug. He's ugh."

"Not at all. He's Gaston, the grand *boulevardier*."

"Everybody hollers when a bug comes out of an apple, but you don't holler or anything."

"Of course not. How would we like it if somebody hollered every time we came out of our house?"

"Why should they?"

"Precisely. So why should we holler at Gaston?"

"He's not the same as us."

"Well, not exactly, but he's the same as a lot of other occupants of peach seeds. Now, the poor fellow hasn't got a home, and there he is with all that pure design and handsome form, and nowhere to go."

195

"Handsome?"

"Gaston is just about the handsomest of his kind I've ever seen."

"What's he saying?"

"Well, he's a little confused. Now, inside that house of his he had everything in order. Bed here, porch there, etc."

"Show me."

The man picked up the peach, leaving Gaston entirely alone on the white plate. He removed the peeling and ate the rest of the peach.

"Nobody else I know would do that," the girl said. "They'd throw it away."

"I can't imagine why. It's a perfectly good peach." He opened the seed and placed the two sides not far from Gaston. The girl studied the open halves.

"Is that where he lives?"

"It's where he used to live. Gaston is out in the world and on his own now. You can see for yourself how comfortable he was in there. He had everything."

"Now what has he got?"

"Not very much, I'm afraid."

"What's he going to do?"

"What are we going to do?"

"Well, we're not going to squash him, that's one thing we're not going to do," the girl said.

"What are we going to do, then?"

"Put him back?"

"Oh, that house is finished."

"Well, he can't live in our house, can he?"

"Not happily."

"Can he live in our house at all?"

"Well, he could try, I suppose. Don't you want a peach?"

"Only if it's a peach with somebody in the seed."

"Well, see if you can find a peach that has an opening at the top, because if you can, that'll be a peach in which you're likeliest to find somebody."

The girl examined each of the peaches on the big plate.

"They're all shut," she said.

"Well, eat one, then."

"No. I want the same kind that you ate, with somebody in the seed."

"Well, to tell you the truth, the peach I ate would be considered a bad peach, so of course stores don't like to sell them. I was sold that one by mistake, most likely. And so now Gaston is without a home, and we've got six perfect peaches to eat."

"I don't want a perfect peach. I want one with people."

"Well, I'll go out and see if I can find one."

"Where will I go?"

"You'll go with me, unless you'd rather stay. I'll only be five minutes."

"If the phone rings, what shall I say?"

"I don't think it'll ring, but if it does, say hello and see who it is."

"If it's my mother, what shall I say?"

"Tell her I've gone to get you a bad peach, and anything else you want to tell her."

"If she wants me to go back, what shall I say?"

"Say yes if you want to go back."

"Do you want me to?"

"Of course not, but the important thing is what you want, not what I want."

"Why is that the important thing?"

"Because I want you to be where you want to be."

"I want to be here."

"I'll be right back."

He put on socks and shoes, and a jacket, and went out.

She watched Gaston trying to find out what to do next. Gaston wandered around the plate, but everything seemed wrong and he didn't know what to do or where to go.

The telephone rang and her mother said she was sending the chauffeur to pick her up because there was a little party for somebody's daughter who was also six, and then tomorrow they would fly back to New York.

"Let me speak to your father," she said.

"He's gone to get a peach."

"One peach?"

"One with people."

"You haven't been with your father two days and already you sound like him."

"There are peaches with people in them. I know. I saw one of them come out."

"A bug?"

"Not a bug. Gaston."

"Who?"

"Gaston the grand something."

"Somebody else gets a peach with a bug in it and throws it away, but not him. He makes up a lot of foolishness about it."

"It's not foolishness."

"All right, all right, don't get angry at me about a horrible peach bug of some kind."

"Gaston is right here, just outside his broken house, and I'm not angry at you."

"You'll have a lot of fun at the party."

"Okay."

"Are you glad you saw your father?"

"Of course I am."

"Is he funny?"

"Yes."

"Is he crazy?"

"Yes. I mean, no. He doesn't holler when he sees a bug crawling out of a peach seed or anything. He just looks at it carefully. But it is just a bug, isn't it really?"

"That's all it is."

"And we'll have to squash it?"

"That's right. I can't wait to see you, darling. These two days have been like two years to me. Goodbye."

The girl watched Gaston on the plate, and she actually didn't like him. He was all ugh, as he had been in the first place. He didn't have a home anymore and he was wandering around on the white plate and he was silly and wrong and ridiculous and useless and all sorts of other things. She cried a little, but only inside, because long ago she had decided she didn't like crying because if you ever started to cry it seemed as if there was so much to cry about you almost couldn't stop, and she didn't like that at all. The open halves of the peach seed were wrong, too. They were ugly or something. They weren't clean.

The man bought a kilo of peaches but found no flawed peaches among them, so he bought another kilo at another store, and this time there were two that were flawed. He hurried back to his flat and let himself in.

His daughter was in her room, in her best dress.

"My mother phoned," she said, "and she's sending the chauffeur for me because there's another birthday party."

"Another?"

"I mean, there's always a lot of them in New York."

"Will the chauffeur bring you back?"

"No. We're flying back to New York tomorrow."

"Oh."

"I liked being in your house."

"I liked having you here."

"Why do you live here?"

"This is my home."

"It's nice, but it's a lot different from our home."

"Yes, I suppose it is."

"It's kind of like Gaston's house."

"Where is Gaston?"

"I squashed him."

"Really? Why?"

"Everybody squashes bugs and worms."

"Oh. Well. I found you a peach."

"I don't want a peach anymore."

"Okay."

He got her dressed, and he was packing her stuff when the chauffeur arrived. He went down the three flights of stairs with his daughter and the chauffeur, and in the street he was about to hug the girl when he decided he had better not. They shook hands instead, like strangers.

He watched the huge car drive off, then he went around the corner where he took coffee every morning, feeling a little, he thought, like Gaston on the white plate.

# SOUMCHI

*Amos Oz*

PROLOGUE

ON CHANGES

*In which may be found a variety of memories and reflections,
comparisons and conclusions. You may skip them if you'd rather and
pass straight on to Chapter One where my story proper begins.*

Everything changes. My friends and acquaintances,
for example, change curtains and professions, exchange
old homes for new ones, shares for securities, or vice
versa, bicycles for motor bicycles, motor bicycles for cars,
exchange stamps, coins, letters, good mornings, ideas
and opinions: some of them exchange smiles.

In the part of Jerusalem known as Sha'are Hesed there
once lived a bank cashier who, in the course of a
single month, changed his home, his wife, his appearance
(he grew a red moustache and sideburns—also reddish),

202

changed first name and surname, changed sleeping and eating habits; in short, he changed everything. One fine day he even changed his job, became a drummer in a night club instead of a cashier (though actually this was not so much a case of change, more like a sock being turned inside out).

Even while we are reflecting on it, by the way, the world about us is gradually changing too. Though the blue transparency of summer still lies across the land, though it is still hot and the sky still blazes above our heads, yet already, near dusk, you can sense some new coolness—at night comes a breeze and the smell of clouds. And just as the leaves begin to redden and to turn, so the sea becomes a little more blue, the earth a little more brown, even the far-off hills these days look somewhat further away.

Everything.

As for me; aged eleven and two months, approximately, I changed completely, four or five times, in the course of a single day. How then shall I begin my story? With Uncle Zemach or Esthie? Either would do. But I think I'll begin with Esthie.

203

## 1

## IN WHICH LOVE BLOSSOMS

*And in which facts will at last be revealed that have been kept
secret to this day; love and other feelings among them.*

Near us in Zachariah Street lived a girl called Esthie. I loved
her. In the morning, sitting at the breakfast table and eating
a slice of bread, I'd whisper to myself, "Esthie."

To which my father would return: "One doesn't eat with
one's mouth open."

While, in the evenings, they'd say of me: "That crazy boy
has shut himself in the bathroom again and is playing with
water."

Only I was not playing with water at all, merely filling
up the hand basin and tracing her name with my finger
across the waves on its surface. At night sometimes I
dreamed that Esthie was pointing at me in the street,
shouting, "Thief, thief!" And I would be frightened
and begin to run away and she would pursue me;
everyone would pursue me, Bar-Kochba Sochobolski
and Goel Germanski and Aldo and Elie Weingarten,
everyone, the pursuit continuing across empty lots and
backyards, over fences and heaps of rusty junk, among
ruins and down alleyways, until my pursuers began to
grow tired and gradually to lag behind, and at last only
Esthie and I would be left running all alone, reaching
almost together some remote and distant spot, a woodshed,
perhaps, or a washhouse on a roof, or the dark angle

under the stairs of a strange house, and then the dream would become both sweet and terrible—oh, I'd awake at night sometimes and weep, almost, from shame. I wrote two love poems in the black notebook that I lost in the Tel Arza wood. Perhaps it was a good thing I lost it.

But what did Esthie know?

Esthie knew nothing. Or knew and wondered.

For example: once I put my hand up in a geography lesson and stated authoritatively:

"Lake Hula is also known as Lake Soumchi." The whole classroom of course immediately roared with loud and unruly laughter. What I had said was the truth; the exact truth in fact, it's in the encyclopedia. In spite of which, our teacher, Mr. Shitrit, got confused for a moment and interrogated me furiously: "Kindly sum up the evidence by which you support your conclusion." But the class had already erupted, was shouting and screaming from every direction:

"Sum it up, Soumchi, sum it up, Soumchi." While Mr. Shitrit swelled like a frog, grew red in the face and roared as usual:

"Let all flesh be silent!" And then, besides: "Not a dog shall bark!"

After five more minutes the class had quieted down again. But, almost to the end of the eighth grade, I remained Soumchi. I've no ulterior motive in telling you all this. I simply want to stress one significant detail; a note sent to me by Esthie at the end of that same lesson, which read as follows:

*You're nuts. Why do you always have to say things that get
you into trouble? Stop it!*

Only then she had folded over one corner at the bottom
of the note and written in it, very small: *But it doesn't
matter. E.*

So what did Esthie know?

Esthie knew nothing, or perhaps she knew and wondered.
As for me, in no circumstance would it have occurred to me
to hide a love letter in her satchel as Elie Weingarten did in
Nourit's, nor to send her a message via Ra'anana, our class
matchmaker, like Tarzan Bamberger, also to Nourit. Quite
the reverse: this is what I did; on every possible occasion I'd
pull Esthie's plaits; time and again I stuck her beautiful
white jumper to her chair with chewing gum.

Why did I do it? Because. Why not? To show her. And
I'd twist her two thin arms behind her back nearly as hard
as I could, until she started calling me names and scratching
me, yet she never begged for mercy. That's what I did to
Esthie. And worse besides. It was me who first nicknamed
her Clementine (from the song that the English soldiers
at the Schneller Barracks were spreading round Jerusalem
those days: *"Oh my darling, oh my darling, oh my dar-ling
Clementine!"*—the girls in our class, surprisingly, picked it
up quite gleefully, and even at Hanukah six months later,
when everything was over, they were still calling Esthie Tina,
which came from Clementina, which came from
Clementine).

And Esthie? She only had one word for me and she threw
it in my face first thing every morning, before I had even
had time to start making a nuisance of myself:

"Louse"—or else:

"You stink."

Once or twice at the ten o'clock break I very nearly reduced Esthie to tears. For that I was handed punishments by Hemda, our teacher, and took them like a man, tight-lipped and uncomplaining.

And that's how love blossomed, without notable event, until the day after the feast of Shavuot. Esthie wept on my account at the ten o'clock break and I wept on hers at night.

2

WITH ALL HIS HEART AND SOUL

*In which Uncle Zemach goes too far and I set out for the source*
*of the River Zambezi (in the heart of Africa).*

At the feast of Shavuot, Uncle Zemach came from Tel Aviv, bringing me a bicycle as a present. As a matter of fact my birthday falls between the two festivals—of Passover and Shavuot. But in Uncle Zemach's eyes, all festivals are more or less the same, except for the Tree Planting festival which he treats with exceptional respect. He used to say, "At Hanukah we children of Israel are taught in school to be angry with the wicked Greeks. At Purim it's the Persians; at Passover we hate Egypt; at Lag B'omer, Rome. On May Day we demonstrate against England; on the Ninth of Av we fast against Babylon and Rome; on the twentieth of

Tammuz, Herzl and Bialik died; while on the eleventh of Adar we must remember for all eternity what the Arabs did to Trumpedor and his companions at Tel Hai. The Tree Planting festival is the only one where we haven't quarreled with anyone and have no griefs to remember. But it almost always rains then—it does it on purpose."

My Uncle Zemach, they had explained to me, was Grandmother Emilia's eldest son by her first marriage, before she married Grandfather Isidore. Sometimes, when he was staying with us, Uncle Zemach would get me out of bed at half past five in the morning and incite me in a whisper to steal into the kitchen with him and cook ourselves an illicit double omelette. He would have a cheerful, even wicked gleam in his eye on those mornings, behaving just as if he and I were fellow members of some dangerous gang and only temporarily engaged in such a relatively innocent pastime as cooking ourselves illicit double omelettes. But my family generally had a very low opinion of my Uncle Zemach. Like this for instance:

"He was a little *spekulant** by the time he was fourteen in Warsaw, in the Nalevki district, and now here he is, still a *spekulant* in Bugrashov Street in Tel Aviv." Or:

"He hasn't changed an atom. Even the sun can't be bothered to brown him. That's the type he is. And there's nothing whatever we can do about it."

But I regarded that last remark as plain stupid and nasty, as well as unfair. My Uncle Zemach didn't get brown

---

* **spekulant.** Black marketeer. —*Trans.*

because he couldn't and that was all there was to it. Even if they'd made him a lifeguard on the beach he'd have got burnt instead of brown, turned red all over, and begun to peel. This is how he was; a young man still, not tall, and so thin and pale he might have been cut out of paper. His hair was whitish, his eyes red like a rabbit's.

And what did *spekulant* mean anyway? I had no idea at all. But in my own mind translated it more or less as follows:

That even when he lived in Warsaw, Uncle Zemach had used to wear a vest and khaki shorts down to his knees and fall fast asleep with the radio on. And he still had not changed; he still clung to his outlandish habits, wore a vest and khaki shorts down to his knees and fell asleep with the radio on. Even here, in Palestine, in Bugrashov Street, Tel Aviv. Well, I thought, what about it, so what?—what's wrong with that? And anyway, my Uncle Zemach lived in Grusenberg Street, not Bugrashov Street. And anyway, sometimes he would burst out singing very loudly in a voice that mooed and brayed and broke,

*"Oh, show me the way to go home . . ."*

At which they would whisper together, very worried and in Yiddish so that I wouldn't understand, but always with the word *meshuggener,* which I knew meant madman. But though they said this of Uncle Zemach, he struck me rather—when he burst out with this song or any other— as not at all a mad man, but simply very sad.

And sometimes he wasn't sad either. Not at all: quite the reverse, he'd be joyous and funny. For instance, he would sit with my parents and my unmarried Aunt Edna on our balcony at dusk and discuss matters which ought not under any circumstances to have been discussed in front of children.

Bargains and profits, building lots and swindles, shares and *lirot*,* scandals and adulteries in Bohemian circles. Sometimes, until they silenced him furiously, he used dirty language. "Quiet, Wetmark," they would say, "what's the matter with you, are you crazy, have you gone completely out of your mind? The boy's listening to everything and he's no baby anymore."

And the presents he would bring me. He kept on thinking up the most amazing, even outrageous, presents. Once, he brought me a Chinese stamp album that twittered when you opened it. Once, a game like Monopoly, only in Turkish. Once, a black pistol that squirted water in your enemy's face. And once he brought me a little aquarium with a pair of live fish swimming about in it, except they were not a pair, as it turned out, but both indubitably male. Another time, he brought me a dart gun. ("Are you out of your mind, Wetmark? The boy's going to put someone's eye out with that thing, God forbid.") And one winter weekend I got from Uncle Zemach a Nazi bank note— no other boy in our neighborhood had anything like it. ("Now, Wetmark, this time you have really gone too far.") And, on Seder night, he presented me with six white mice in a cage. ("So what else are you going to bring the boy? Snakes? Bedbugs? Cockroaches, perhaps?")

---

* **lirot.** Pounds. — *Trans.*

This time, Uncle Zemach marked the feast of Shavuot by riding all the way from the Egged bus station in the Jaffa Road to the courtyard of our house on a secondhand Raleigh bicycle, complete with every accessory: it had a bell, also a lamp, also a carrier, also a reflector at the back; all it lacked was the crossbar joining the saddle to the handlebars. But, in my first overwhelming joy, I overlooked just how grave a shortcoming that was.

Mother said: "Really, this is excessive, Zemach. The boy is still only eleven. What are you proposing to give him for his Bar Mitzvah?"

"A camel," said Uncle Zemach at once, and with an air of such total indifference, he might have prepared himself for this very question all along.

Father said: "Would it be worth your considering at least once the effects on his education? Seriously, Zemach, where's it all leading to?"

I did not wait for Uncle Zemach's reply. Nor did it matter to me in the least where things were leading. Crazy with pride and joy, I was galloping my bicycle to my private place behind the house. And there, where no one could see me, I kissed its handlebars, then kissed the back of my own hands again and again and, in a whisper as loud as a shout, chanted: "Lord God Almighty, Lord God Almighty, LORD GOD ALMIGHTY." And, afterwards, in a deep, wild groan that broke from the depths of my being: "HI—MA—LA—YA."

And after that, I leaned the bicycle against a tree and leaped high into the air. It was only when I calmed down a little that I noticed Father. He stood in a window above my head and watched in unbroken silence until I had quite finished. Then he said:

"All right. So be it. All I beg is that we should make a little agreement between us. You may ride your new bicycle for up to an hour and a half each day. No more. You'll ride always on the right-hand side, whether there is traffic in the street or not. And you will remain always, exclusively, within the boundaries set by the following streets: Malachi, Zephania, Zachariah, Ovadia, and Amos. You will not enter Geula Street, because it is too full of the comings and goings of the British drivers from the Schneller Barracks; whether they are intoxicated or the enemies of Israel, or both, is immaterial. And at all intersections you will kindly, please, use your intelligence a little."

*"On the wings of eagles,"* said Uncle Zemach.

And Mother added: "Yes, but carefully."

I said: "Fine, goodbye." But when I had gone a little way from them, added: "It will be all right." And went out into the street.

How they stared at me then, the boys of our neighborhood; classmates, big boys, little boys alike. I watched them too, but sideways, so that they wouldn't notice it, and saw envy, mockery, and malice there. But what did I care? Very slowly and deliberately I processed in front of them, not riding my bicycle, but pushing it, one-handed, along the pavement, right under their noses, wearing on my face meanwhile a thoughtful, even smug, expression, as if to ask:

"What's all the fuss about? It's just a Raleigh bicycle. Of course you can do exactly as you like. You can burst on the spot if you like, but it's your own look out. It's got absolutely nothing to do with me."

Indeed, Elie Weingarten could not keep silence any longer. He opened his mouth and said, very coolly, like a scientist identifying some unusual lizard just discovered in a field:

"Just look at this. They've gone and bought Soumchi a girl's bike, without a crossbar."

"Perhaps they'll buy him a party frock next," said Bar-Kochba Sochobolski. He did not even bother to look at me, nor cease tossing deftly up and down two silver coins at once.

"A pink hair ribbon would suit Soumchi very well"— this was the voice of Tarzan Bamberger. "And he and Esthie can be best friends." (Bar-Kochba again.) "Except Esthie wears a bra already and Soumchi doesn't need one yet." (Elie Weingarten, the skunk.)

That was it. Enough, I decided. More than enough. Finish.

I did not start calling them names nor set about breaking their bones one by one. Instead I made them the same rude gesture with my left thumb that Uncle Zemach made whenever the name of the British Foreign Minister, Bevin, was mentioned, turned around instantly, and rode off on my bicycle down Zephania Street.

Let them say anything they liked.

Let them burst in a million pieces.

What should I care?

Besides, on principle, I never pick a fight with boys weaker than myself. And, besides, what was all this about

Esthie suddenly? What made them think of Esthie? Right then. It was still daylight. I would set off here and now on my bicycle for faraway places, head south on the Katamon and Talpiot Road, and on farther, via Bethlehem, Hebron, and Beersheva, via the Negev and Sinai deserts, towards the heart of Africa and the source of the River Zambezi, there to brave alone a mob of bloodthirsty savages.

But I had barely reached the end of Zephania Street when I began to ask myself: Why do they hate me so, those bastards? And knew, suddenly, in my heart of hearts that it was my fault just as much as theirs. I felt an instant sense of relief. After all, an ability to show mercy even to his worst enemy is the mark of a great and noble soul. No power in all the world, no possible obstacle could deter such a man from traveling to the farthest frontiers of unknown lands. I would go now to consult Aldo, I decided, and afterwards, this very day and without more ado, would continue on my journey to Africa.

## 3

## WHO SHALL ASCEND
## UNTO THE HILL OF THE LORD?

*In which negotiations are concluded, a contract signed,
and a number of plans discussed, as are faraway places where no
white man has ever set foot.*

In the last house but one in Zephania Street lived my friend, Aldo Castelnuovo, whose father was famous for his conjuring tricks with matches and playing cards; besides which he owned a large travel agency, *The Orient Express*. I knew that Aldo, of all people, must see my new bicycle. It was the one thing his parents had not bought him, though they had bought him almost everything else. They would not allow Aldo a bicycle because of the various dangers involved and, in particular, because it might hinder Aldo's progress on the violin. It was for this reason that I whistled to Aldo furtively, from outside his house. When Aldo appeared he took the situation in at a glance, managing to smuggle the bicycle quickly into a disused shed in their back garden without his mother having suspected anything at all.

Afterwards, we both went into the house and shut ourselves up in Aldo's father's library (Professor Emilio Castelnuovo having gone to Cairo for four days on business). It greeted me, as usual, with a smell both gloomy and enticing, made up of muttered secrets and hushed carpets, stealthy plots and leather upholstery, illicit whisperings and distant journeys. All day long, all summer long, the library shutters were kept closed to prevent sunlight fading the beautiful leather bindings with their gold-lettered spines.

We took out the huge German atlas and compared carefully every possible route on the map of Africa. Aldo's mother sent the Armenian nanny, Louisa, to us with a dish full of nuts—peanuts and almonds, walnuts and sunflower seeds—also orange juice in delicate blue glasses, still sweating with cold.

When we had demolished the peanuts and walnuts and begun on the sunflower seeds, the conversation turned to bicycles in general and my bicycle in particular. If Aldo were secretly to own a bicycle of his own, it should be possible, we decided, to keep it hidden from all suspicious eyes, at the back of the disused shed. And then, early on Saturday mornings, while his parents were still safely fast asleep, he would be able to creep out; there would be nothing to stop him riding right to the end of the world.

I pronounced expert opinions on a thousand and one relevant items, approving or disapproving of them accordingly. On spokes and valves and safety valves; on batteries as compared to dynamos; on handbrakes (which, applied at speed, would send you flying immediately) as against back pedal brakes (let them go on a downhill slope and you might as well start saying your prayers); on ordinary carriers as compared to spring carriers; on lamps and reflectors; and so on and so forth. Afterwards, we returned to the subject of the Zulu and the Bushmen and the Hottentot, what each tribe had in common and in which way each one was unique, and which of them was the most dangerous. I spoke, eagerly, about the terrible Mahdi of Khartoum in the capital city of Sudan, about the real, original Tarzan from the forests of Tanganyika, through which I would have to pass on my journey to the source of the River Zambezi in the land of Obangi-Shari. But Aldo was not listening anymore. He was miles away, deep in his own thoughts and seemed to grow more nervous every minute. Suddenly he cut me short, and, in a voice high and trembling with excitement, burst out:

"Come on! Come to my room: I'll show you something better than you've dreamed in all your life!"

"OK. But quick," I begged. "I've got to get started on my journey today."

Yet, even so I followed him out of the library. To reach Aldo's room meant traversing almost the entire length of the Castelnuovos' house. It was very large, all its carpets and curtains spotlessly clean, yet contriving at one and the same time to be both faintly gloomy and a touch exotic. In the sitting room, for instance, there was a brown grandfather clock with golden hands and square Hebrew letters instead of numbers. There were low cupboards along the walls and on top of them rows and rows of small antiques made of wood or solid silver. There was even a silver crocodile, but its tail was no ordinary tail—it acted as a lever also. If you pulled it and then pressed very lightly the crocodile would crack nuts between its jaws for the benefit of the Castelnuovos' guests. Moreover, the door of the passageway between the drawing room and the oblong dining room was guarded balefully night and day by

Caesario, a large woolen dog, stuffed with seaweed and glowering at you with black buttons in place of eyes.

In the dining room itself stood an enormous table made of mahogany, wearing what looked like felt stockings on each of its thick legs. And on the wall of the dining room in letters of gold, this inscription appeared: *Who shall ascend unto the hill of the Lord? Who shall stand in His holy place?* The answer to that question, *He who has clean hands and a pure heart*—which happened also to be the Castelnuovo family motto—was to be found on the opposite wall encircling the family crest; a single blue gazelle, each of its horns a Star of David.

From the dining room, a glass door led to a little cubbyhole called "The Smoking Room." An enormous painting hid one wall entirely. It showed a woman in a delicate muslin dress, a silk scarf concealing all her face except for her two black eyes, while, with one white hand, she held out to a beggar a golden coin so bright and shining it sprayed small sparks in all directions, like sparks from a fire. But the beggar himself continued to sit there peacefully. He wore a clean white cloak, his beard too was white, his eyes closed, his face radiant with happiness. Beneath the picture on a small copper plaque was engraved the single word, *CHARITY.*

I marveled so often in this house. At Louisa, for instance, the Armenian nanny who looked after Aldo; a dark and very polite girl of sixteen or seventeen whom I never saw without a clean white apron on top of her blue dress, both dress and apron looking newly ironed. She could talk Italian with Aldo, yet obeyed his order without question.

She was also exceedingly courteous to me, calling me "the young gentleman," in a strange, almost dreamlike, Hebrew until sometimes, even to myself, I began to seem like a real young gentleman. Could she be the daughter of the woman in that great picture in the smoking room; and if not, why the likeness between them? And then, was *CHARITY* the name of the picture? Or the name of the woman in the picture? Or even the name of the painter who had painted it? Our teacher in Class Two had been called Margolit Charity. It was she who had given Aldo the Hebrew name "Alded." But who could give a name like Alded to a boy in whose house there was a room just for smoking?

(My parents' flat, with its two rooms and kitchen, separated by a short corridor, had only plain wooden tables and rush-seated chairs. Anemones or sprays of almond blossom flowered there in yogurt jars in spring, while in summer and autumn the same jars sprouted branches of myrtle. The picture on the wall of the larger of our rooms showed a pioneer carrying a hoe and looking, for no obvious reason, towards a row of cypresses.)

At the far end of the smoking room was a strange low door. We went through it and down five steps to the wing of the house which contained Aldo's room. His window looked out on the crowded red roofs of the Mea Shearim quarter, and beyond them, eastwards, onto church towers and mountains.

"Now," said Aldo, as if about to perform some kind of magic, "now, just take a look at this."

And at that, he bent down and pulled from a large and brightly patterned box, section after section of dismantled railway track, several small stations, and a railway official made of tin. There followed the most marvelous blue engine, with a quantity of red carriages. Then we laid ourselves down on the floor and began to put it all together, the track layout, the signaling system, even the scenery. (It too was made of brightly painted tin; hills and bridges, lakes and tunnels; tiny cows had even been painted on the hillsides, grazing peacefully alongside the steep track.)

And when at last all was ready, Aldo connected the electric plug and the whole enchanted world sprang instantly to life. Engines whistled, coach wheels clicked busily along the tracks, barriers went up and came down again, signal lights flashed intermittently at crossings and interchanges; goods trains and passenger trains, exchanging hoots of greeting, passed or overtook each other on parallel rails—magic upon magic, enchantment on enchantment.

"This," said Aldo with a slight disdain, "this I got as a present from my godfather, Maestro Enrico. He's Viceroy of Venezuela now." I was silent with awe.

But in my heart I was thinking:

Lord God Almighty. King of the Universe.

"As far as I am concerned," added Aldo with indifference, "the whole thing's pretty boring. Not to say a waste of time. Myself, I'd rather play my violin than play with toys these days. So you might as well have it. If you still play with toys, that is."

"Hallelujah, Hallelujah," my soul sang within my breast. But I still said nothing.

"Of course—" Aldo grew more precise, "—of course, I don't mean as a present. As a swap. In exchange for your bicycle. Do you agree?"

Wow, I thought to myself. Wow. And how. But out loud, I said, "OK. Done. Why not?"

"And of course," went on Aldo immediately, "of course I don't mean the whole thing. Just one section of it in exchange for your bike; one engine, that is, five carriages, and three meters of circular track. After all, your bike doesn't have a crossbar. What I'm going to do now is fetch a blank contract from Father's drawer, and if you haven't had second thoughts and changed your mind—which you still have a perfect right to do—we can sign it there and then and shake hands on it. In the meantime, you may start choosing the amount of track and the number of carriages that we agreed, plus your one engine—one of the small ones of course, not the large. I'll be back in a minute. *Ciao.*"

But I was not listening anymore. I couldn't hear anything except my own heart galloping away inside my breast and bellowing out: "Shoe—shoe—shoe—shoe—shoey-shoe" (which was a nonsense song absolutely everyone was singing in those days).

In a minute the contract had been signed and I had left the Castelnuovos' house, bursting out into Zephania Street like a train out of a tunnel, carrying carefully in front of me a shoebox gift-wrapped and tied up with blue ribbon. To judge by the light and the coolness of the air, it was half an hour or so till dusk and suppertime. I would set out the railway, I thought, in the wild and untamed landscape of our garden. I would dig a winding river, I thought, and fill it with water and make the railway cross it on a bridge. I'd raise hills and scoop out valleys, run a tunnel beneath the hanging roots of the fig tree and from there my new railway would erupt into the wilderness itself, into the barren Sahara and beyond, up to the source of the River Zambezi in the land of Obangi-Shari, through deserts and impenetrable forests where no white man had ever set foot.

4

YOUR MONEY OR YOUR LIFE

*In which we confront an old enemy, a bitter and cunning foe,*
*who will stop at nothing. To avoid unnecessary bloodshed,*
*we are obliged to fight our way through a thicket of intrigue and*
*even to tame a young wild beast.*

To judge from the fading light and cooler air, night and suppertime were approaching fast. At the corner of Jonah Street I stopped for a moment to read a new inscription on the wall. Two mornings ago it had been empty, but here now in black paint was a fierce slogan against the British and David Ben-Gurion. It was such a silly, irritating slogan in fact, even the spelling mistake seemed shocking.

> *British go hom*
> *Get out Ben Gurion*

I identified its author immediately. Goel. For this was no slogan from the Underground. This had to be the work of

222

Goel Germanski himself. Having determined which, I took out a notebook and pencil and started to copy the inscription down. I need to make a note of everything like that, since I am going to be a poet when I grow up.

I was still standing there, writing, when Goel himself appeared. Large and silent, he crept up behind me, moving as precisely as a wolf in a forest. He grabbed my shoulders in his two strong hands and did not let me go. I did not struggle. For one thing, I don't, on principle, pick fights with boys stronger than myself. For another, I had not forgotten that I was clutching my railway, my dearest possession, in a box beneath my arm. Consequently, I needed to take particular care.

Goel Germanski was our class hoodlum, our neighborhood hoodlum, you could say. He was very tough and muscular, the son of the deputy headmaster of our school. His mother, it was rumored, "worked in Haifa for the French." Since our heavy defeat at Purim at the hands of the Bokarim Quarter, we had been enemies, Goel and I. These days we did talk to each other, even went so far as to discuss our defeat, but always using the third person. And if I saw on Goel a certain ominous smile, I would do my best to be found on the opposite side of the street. For Goel's smile said this, approximately:

"Everyone except you knows that something very nasty is about to get you; any time now you'll know it too; all the rest of us will be laughing, only you will be laughing on the other side of your face."

Meanwhile, Goel had gripped my shoulders and asked, smiling, "So what's his little game then?"

"Please let me go," I begged politely. "It's late and I'm already supposed to be back home."

"Is that so then?" inquired Goel, letting go my shoulder. But he did not stop staring at me suspiciously, as if I had said something amazingly cunning; yet, if I had hoped thereby to fool Goel Germanski himself, then I had another think coming. That was how Goel looked at me.

Then he added very quietly:

"So he wants to go home, huh."

It was no question the way he said it. It was more as if he was pointing at some nasty aspect of my character which he was only just discovering, much to his sorrow and disappointment.

"I'm late already," I explained gently.

"Just get an earful of this," cried Goel to some invisible audience. "So he's late, huh? So all at once he wants to go home, huh? He's nothing but a dirty British spy, that's all he is. But as from right now we've got him fixed, him and his informing. As from right now we've fixed him for good."

"To start with," I corrected him cautiously, my heart pounding under my T-shirt, "to start with, I'm not a spy."

"So he isn't, is he?" winked Goel, simultaneously friendly and malevolent. "So how come he's copying that stuff from the wall, how come?"

"So what?" I inquired. And then, with a burst of courage, added: "The street doesn't belong to him. The street's public property."

"That's what he thinks," explained Goel, with a schoolmasterly patience, "that's what he thinks. Because right now he's going to start opening up that parcel of his and letting us take a good look inside."

"No I'm not."

"Open up."

"No."

"For the third and last time. He'll open up. If he knows what's good for him. That Soumchi. That scab. That dirty British spy. He'll open up, and fast, else I'll give him a hand right now."

So I untied the blue ribbon, removed the fine wrappings, revealed to Goel Germanski my railway, in all its glory.

After a brief, awed silence, Goel said, "And is he going to tell me he got all that from Sergeant Dunlop? Just for informing and nothing else?"

"I'm not an informer. I teach Sergeant Dunlop Hebrew sometimes and he teaches me English. That's all. I'm not an informer."

"Then how come the railway? How come the engine? Unless, maybe, this well-known benefactor suddenly started handing out goodies to the poor?"

"It's none of his business," I said in the ensuing silence, heroically.

In return, Goel Germanski grabbed hold of my T-shirt and shook me against the fence, two or three times. He did not shake me savagely but delicately rather—I might have been a winter coat from which he was trying to remove dust and the smell of mothballs.

And when he had quite finished, he inquired anxiously, as though concerned for my welfare, "Maybe he's ready to do some talking now?"

"OK," I said. "OK. OK. If he'll let go of me. I swapped it. If he must know."

"He wouldn't be lying by any chance?" Goel sounded suspicious suddenly, wore on his face an expression of the deepest moral concern.

"Cross my heart. It's the absolute truth," I swore. "I swapped it with Aldo. There's even a contract in my pocket to prove it. Then he can see for himself. I swapped it for the bike I got from my uncle."

"Uncle Wetmark," Goel pointed out.

"Uncle Zemach," I corrected him.

"A girl's bike," said Goel.

"With a lamp and a dynamo," I insisted.

"Aldo Castelnuovo?" said Goel.

"As a swap," I said. "Here's the contract."

"Right," said Goel. And thereafter looked thoughtful. We were silent for a little while. In the sky, and outside, in the courtyard, it was still daylight. But I could smell the evening approaching now. Goel broke the silence at last.

"Right," he said. "He's made one swap. Now here's another for him, if he wants. Psssst. Keeper. Here: down, sit! Sit! Right, like that. Good dog. Yes, you are. This is Keeper; he'd better take a good look at him before he makes up his mind. There's no dog like him today. Not even for fifty pounds apiece. They don't sell dogs with such pedigrees any more. His father belongs to King Farouk of Egypt; his mother to Esther Williams, in the pictures."

At Goel's shrill whistle and the sound of the name Keeper, a very young and enthusiastic Alsatian had sprung from the nearest courtyard and begun prancing all around us, panting and yelping and leaping and quivering, dancing with happiness, exploding with excitement, still so nearly a puppy he waggled his whole hindquarters, instead of just his tail. He fawned and fawned on Goel: he pressed himself against him, as if attempting to implant himself; begged his attention, to stay with him forever; flattered and beseeched him; clambered over him, his paws trembling with joy, his eyes firing sparks of wolfish love at him. In the end he was standing on his hind legs, scrabbling with all his might at Goel's stomach, until Goel checked him suddenly, with a masterful, "That's enough! Sit!"

In an instant, Keeper's lovemaking had come to an abrupt halt. His manner changed completely. He sat himself down, folding his tail neatly about him, expression thoughtful, even smug. He held his back, his head, his muzzle, as tense and still as if he were balancing a shilling on the end of his black nose. His furry ears were pricked. He was wrapped in such total gravity and humility; he looked so like a newly-arrived immigrant boy, a particularly clean and tidy boy, trying his hardest to please, it was almost impossible not to burst out laughing.

"Die," roared Goel, huskily.

Instantly Keeper prostrated himself at his feet and threw his head on his paws in eternal submission. His grief was as delicate as a poet's. His tail lay motionless, his ears were limp and totally despairing, he appeared to have ceased to breathe. Still, when Goel broke a small branch from a mulberry tree behind the fence, Keeper did not move; did not even blink an eye. And only the faintest of tremblings flowed along his back and made his gray-brown fur quiver.

But when, suddenly, Goel threw the stick into the distance and yelled "Fetch!" in a stern voice, the dog sprang, instantly—no, did not spring, erupted—like a shower of sparks out of a bonfire, parting the air, describing four or five wide arcs on it—he might in his fury have sprouted invisible wings. His wolf's jaw opened—I caught one brief glimpse of a red-black gullet, of white teeth sharpened for the kill—the next minute Keeper was back from his errand and laying the stick at his master's feet. Then he too laid himself down in mute, even slavish submission, as if confessing that he was fit for nothing so demanded nothing, except to fulfill his obligations, naturally, for what's one caress between you and me in the end?

"Well, that's it," said Goel.

While the dog lifted his head and looked up at him with eyes full of longing and barely-concealed love, that asked:

"Am I a good dog then?"

"Yes," said Goel. "Yes, a very good dog. But you're going to change masters now. And if he doesn't treat Keeper well—" though Goel was addressing me now he still did not look at me, "—If he doesn't treat Keeper well, I'll kill him on the spot, I'll kill him; get that, Soumchi?"

He spoke these last words in a menacing whisper, his face thrust close up to mine.

"Me?" I asked, hardly daring to believe my ears.

"Yes, him," said Goel. "He's getting Keeper, as from now. And then I'll know for sure he's not an informer."

The dog was still only a puppy, though no longer helpless and no longer little. He'll obey my voice,

I thought. And how. And I'll turn him back into a proper wolf, a real fierce proper wolf.

"Has he ever read *The Hound of the Baskervilles*?" asked Goel.

"Of course I have," I said. "At least twice, if not three times."

"Good. Then he'd better know this dog's been trained to tear throats out too. British cops' and spies' throats. At a word of command. And that word's the name of the King of England—I won't say it now or he'll start attacking someone here."

"Of course," I said.

"And on top of that, he'll take messages anywhere he's sent. And track down a suspect just from sniffing at one of his socks," added Goel. And after a short silence, as if he was having to make a difficult and painful decision, muttered: "Right. OK. He gets Keeper. In exchange, that is. As a swap. Not for free. For the railway."

"But . . ."

"And if he won't, I'll show the whole class the love poem he wrote Esthie Inbar in the black notebook Aldo stole from the pocket of his windcheater in the Tel Arza wood."

"Bastards," I hissed, between gritted teeth. "Contemptible bastards." (Contemptible was a word I'd learned from Uncle Zemach.)

Goel found it expedient to ignore these epithets and preserve his good humor. "If he'll let me finish; before he starts swearing at me. Whatever that was all about. If he'll just let someone else say something. If he'll just keep his cool. He'll not only get Keeper in exchange, he'll get back his black notebook, and as well as that, he can join the Avengers, and as well as that I'll make peace with him. He only has to think a bit and he'll know what's good for him."

At that very moment a delicious haze spread through my body. Excitement gently stroked my back; there was a melting in my throat and my knees were trembling with delight.

"Hang on," I protested, at the sight of Goel beginning to untie the blue ribbons from the railway box and improvise a lead for Keeper. "Hang on, hang on a minute."

"There you are, Soumchi." Goel actually addressed me in the second person as if we were friends again, as if nothing had happened at Purim in the battle with the Bokarim Quarter, as if suddenly I was just like anybody else.

"There you are. Grab him. Only you've got to be firm with him. He might try and escape at first, until he gets used to you. Until he does, don't let him off the lead. In a few days he'll do just what you tell him. Just do me a personal favor, though, treat him properly. And tomorrow, at three o'clock, come to the secret place on Tarzan Bamberger's roof. On the stairs you'll have to tell Bar-Kochba the password, 'Lily of the Valley,' and wait for him to answer 'Rose of Sharon,' then you'll say 'Rivers of Egypt' and he'll let you past. Because those are the Avengers' passwords. And then you'll be sworn in and then you'll get your notebook back with those poems I was talking about; I forget what they were about. Right. That's the lot. Just come tomorrow at three o'clock, or else. Go on, Keeper. Go with Soumchi. Go on, pull him, Soumchi. Pull him hard, like that. So long."

"So long, Goel," I answered, as if I really was just like anybody else, though actually, inside my head, my soul went on singing over and over like some demented songbird, "I've got a wolf, I've got a wolf, I've got a young wolf to tear out throats." But it took all my strength to drag my reluctant wolf cub after me. He dug his paws into the cracks in the pavement, protesting his wretchedness meanwhile with pathetic little whines that were beneath him altogether. So I ignored them. I just kept pulling him along. I pulled and walked and walked and pulled, while my spirit was borne far, far away, to the tangled forests and impenetrable jungles, where, surrounded, I made a brave and hopeless stand against a mob of shrieking cannibals, covered in war paint and brandishing javelins and spears. Alone and weaponless, I struck out on all sides, but for every one of them I felled with my bare hands, a host of others swarmed yelling from their lair to take his place. Already my strength was beginning to fail. But then, as my enemies closed in on me with cries of joy, their white teeth gleaming, I gave one short, shrill whistle. From out of the thicket leaped my own private wolf, menacing, merciless, rending their throats with his cruel fangs until my enemies had scattered in all directions, bellowing with fear. Then he flung himself down at my feet and lay there panting, fawning on me and looking up at me with hidden love and longing, as if to say:

"Am I a good dog?"

"Yes, a very good dog," I said. But deep in my heart I thought: This is happiness; and that's life. Here is love and here am I.

And, afterwards, darkness fell and we continued on our way through the gloom of the jungle to the source of the River Zambezi in the land of Obangi-Shari, where no white man had ever set foot, and to which my heart goes out.

5

## TO HELL WITH EVERYTHING

*In which King Saul loses his father's asses and then finds a kingdom; and in which we too lose and find: and in which evening descends on Jerusalem and a fateful decision is reached.*

The street was already darkening and it was growing late. Somehow I managed to drag the young wolf I got from Goel Germanski in exchange for an electric railway as far as the junction of Zephania and Malachi Streets. But there, just by the postbox, set into the concrete wall, painted bright red, with a crown raised on it and underneath the initials, in English, of King George, the dog decided he had had enough. He pulled so hard, perhaps at the sound of some whistle I could not hear, he tore off the lead that Goel Germanski had made him out of the blue gift ribbon, so freeing himself. Then he crossed the road at a crouching run, his tail between his legs and his muzzle close to the ground, very furtive-looking, almost reptilian. Thereafter, he crept along, keeping his distance from me, as if admitting that such behavior was disgraceful. Yet, claiming too, in his own defense:

"That's how it is, mate. That's life, I'm afraid."

And then he was gone from my sight altogether, vanished into the darkness of one of the courtyards.

Night fell.

And so that bad dog had returned quite certainly to his real master. And what was I left with? Just one small length of the blue ribbon that Aldo Castelnuovo had tied round the box that held the railway that Goel Germanski had converted into a lead for his dog. Otherwise, I was empty-handed, and also quite alone. But that was life.

By now, I had reached the courtyard of the Faithful Remnant Synagogue (which happened to be my shortcut home, via the Bambergers' butcher's shop). I did not hurry. I had no reason to hurry anymore. On the contrary. I sat down on a box and listened to the sounds about me and began to set myself to thinking. Around and around flowed the warmth and peace of early evening. I heard the sound of radios from open windows, the sound of voices, laughing or scolding. Since it no longer mattered to anyone what would happen to me—not now or all the rest of my life—it did not matter much to me what would happen to anybody else. Yet, in spite of that, I felt sorry, at that moment, because everything in the world kept changing and nothing ever stayed the same, and sorry even that this evening would never come again, though I had no reason to love this evening. On the contrary, in fact. Yet I still felt sorry for what was and would not be a second time. And I wondered if there was some faraway place somewhere in the world, in Obangi-Shari perhaps, or among the Himalayan mountains, where it might be possible to order time not to keep on passing and light not to keep on changing, just as they had been ordered by Joshua, son of Nun, in the Book of Joshua. At which, someone on one of the balconies called her neighbor a crazy fool and the neighbor answered for her part, "Just look who's talking. Mrs. Rotloi. Mrs. *Rotloi*." And afterwards followed some garbled, incomprehensible sentences, in Polish maybe. And suddenly a fearful shriek rose from Zachariah Street—for a moment I hoped that Red Indians had started to attack the neighborhood already and were mercilessly scalping the inhabitants. But it was only a cat that cried and he only cried for love.

And among all the sounds of evening came the smells of evening; the smell of sauerkraut and tar and cooking oil, of souring rubbish in rubbish bins, and the smell of warm, wet washing hung out to catch the evening breeze. Because it was evening, in Jerusalem.

While I, for my part, sat on an empty box in the courtyard of the Faithful Remnant Synagogue, wondering why I should keep trying to deny it all, about Esthie.

Esthie; who is, at this moment, quite certainly sitting in her room, which I'd never seen, nor was ever likely to. And equally certainly will have drawn her two blue curtains (with which, on the other hand, I was extremely well acquainted, having looked at them from the outside a thousand times and more). And is most probably doing the homework that I have forgotten to touch, answering in her round hand the simple questions set by Mr. Shitrit, the geography teacher. Or maybe untying her plaits, or rearranging them, or maybe, very patiently, cutting out decorations for the end of term party; her skirt stretched tightly across her lap; her nails clean and rounded, not black and split like mine. She is breathing very quietly—just as in class her lips will not quite be closed and every now and then she'll be trying to reach some imaginary speck on her upper lip with the tip of her tongue. I cannot tell what she is thinking about; except that certainly she is not thinking about me. And if something does happen to remind her of me, it is most likely as "that disgusting Soumchi"; or "that crazy boy." Better, therefore, she does not think of me at all.

And, anyway, that was quite enough of that. Better for me too to stop thinking about Esthie and instead start considering, very carefully, a much more urgent question.

I began to collect up my thoughts, just as my father had taught me to do at some moment of decision. He had taught me to set down on paper all possible courses of action, together with their pros and cons, erasing one by one the least promising of them, then grading the rest according to a points' system. However, a pencil would be no use now, with daylight already gone. Instead, I listed the various alternatives in my head, as follows:

A.   I could get up and go straight home, explaining my being late and empty-handed on the grounds that my bicycle had been stolen or else confiscated by some drunken British soldier, and I had not resisted him because my mother had ordered me not to argue with the soldiers, ever.

B.   I could go back to Aldo's. Louisa, the Armenian nanny, would open the door to me and tell me to wait one moment. Then she would go by herself to announce that the young gentleman had returned and wanted a word with our young gentleman, and afterwards, very politely, she would usher me to the room where the magnificent lady in the muslin dress was presenting the beggar with a golden coin. And then I would have to confess to Aldo's mother that I had let Aldo have a bicycle, had even signed a contract for it. At which Aldo's mother would certainly punish him severely, because, under no circumstances, was he supposed to have a bicycle. And I would have behaved like a dirty low informer and not even got my bicycle back for my pains, since I no longer had the railway. Out of the question.

C. I could return to Goel Germanski. And announce in a very cold and ominous voice that he was to return the railway immediately, our contract being canceled. That he'd better give it back or I'd finish him for good. Yes, but how?

D. I could still return to Goel Germanski. But apparently friendly. "Hello, how are you, how's things?" And then ask casually if Keeper has come back to him by any chance? Yes. Of course. And tomorrow the joke will be all round the neighborhood. Total disgrace.

E. Who needs the wretched dog in any case? Who needs anything? I don't. So there. Anyway, who says Keeper fled straight back to Goel Germanski's? More likely he had run in the darkness to the Tel Arza wood and then on to the barren hills and then on to the forests of Galilee to join the rest of the pack in the wild and so to lead the life of a real free wolf at last, tearing out throats with his fangs.

Perhaps, right now, at this moment, I too could get to my feet and go to the Tel Arza wood; and from there to

236

the hills and the caves and the winds to live as a bandit all the rest of my life and spread the fear of my name through the land forever.

Or, I could go home, tell, humbly, the whole truth, get my face slapped a few times and promise faithfully that from now on I would be a well-behaved and sensible boy instead of a crazy one. Then, straightaway, I would be dispatched with polite and apologetic notes from my father to Mrs. Castelnuovo and Mr. Germanski. I would apologize in my turn; assure everyone I hadn't really meant it; would smile a stupid smile and beg everyone's pardon; tell everyone how sorry I was for everything that had happened. Quite out of the question.

F? G? H? Never mind. But a further possibility was simply to fall asleep among the ruins just like Huckleberry Finn in *The Adventures of Tom Sawyer.* I'd spend the night under the steps of the Inbars' house; in the very dead of night I'd climb the drainpipe to Esthie's room and we'd elope together to the land of Obangi-Shari before the crack of dawn.

But Esthie hates me. Perhaps worse than hates, she never thinks of me at all.

One last possibility. At Passover, I'd gone in Sergeant Dunlop's jeep to an Arab village and never told my parents anything. Well now, I could go to Aunt Edna's in the Yegia Capiim neighborhood, look unhappy, tell her Father and Mother had gone to Beit Hakerem this morning to visit friends and wouldn't be back till late, so they'd left me a key, and, well, I didn't quite know how to put this, only, well, I seem to have lost it, and . . . But, oh, that Aunt

Edna, who wore imitation fruit in her hair and had a house full of paper flowers and ornaments and never stopped kissing me and fussing over me . . . and . . . Never mind. It would have to do. At least it solved the problem for tonight. And by tomorrow Mother and Father would be so out of their minds with worry and so thankful to see me safe and well, they would quite forget to ask what had happened to my bicycle.

Right. Let's go. I got to my feet, having made up my mind at last to beg shelter at my Aunt Edna's in the Yegia Capiim neighborhood. Only there was something glittering in the dark among the pine needles. I bent to the ground, straightened up again, and there it was, a pencil sharpener.

Not a large pencil sharpener. And not exactly new. Yet made of metal, painted silver, and heavy for its size, cool-feeling and pleasant to my hand. A pencil sharpener. That I could sharpen pencils with, but also make serve as a tank in the battles that I fought out with buttons on the carpet.

And so, I tightened my fingers round my pencil sharpener, turned and ran straight for home, because I wasn't empty-handed anymore.

# SOUMCHI

*Amos Oz*

6

### ALL IS LOST

*"We'll never set foot . . ." In which I resolve to climb the Mountains
of Moab and gaze upon the Himalayas, receive a surprising invitation
(and determine not to open my hand, not as long as I shall live).*

Father asked softly:

"Do you know what time it is?"

"Late," I said sadly. And gripped my pencil sharpener harder.

"The time is now seven thirty-six," Father pointed out. He stood, blocking the doorway, and nodded his head many times, as if he had reached that sad but inevitable conclusion there and then. He added: "We have already eaten."

"I'm sorry," I muttered, in a very small voice.

239

"We have not only eaten. We have washed up the dishes," revealed Father, quietly. There was another silence. I knew very well what was to follow. My heart beat and beat.

"And just where has his lordship been all this time? And just where is his bicycle?"

"My bicycle?" I said, dismayed. And the blood rushed from my face.

"The bicycle," repeated Father patiently, stressing each syllable precisely. "The bicycle."

"My bicycle," I muttered after him, stressing each syllable exactly as he did. "My bicycle. Yes. It's at my friend's house. I left it with one of my friends." And my lips went on whispering of their own accord, "Until tomorrow."

"Is that so?" returned Father sympathetically, as if he shared my suffering wholeheartedly and was about to offer me some plain but sound advice. "Perhaps I might be permitted to know the name and title of this honored friend?"

"That," I said, "that, I am unable to reveal."

"No?"

"No."

"Under no circumstance?"

"Under no circumstance."

It was now, I knew, he'd let fly with the first slap. I shrank right back, as if I was trying to bury my head between my shoulders, my whole body inside my shoes, shut my eyes, and gripped my pencil sharpener with all my might. I took three or four breaths and waited. But no slap came. I opened my eyes and blinked. Father stood there, looking sorrowful, as if he was waiting for the performance to be over. At last he said,

"Just one more question. If his lordship will kindly permit."

"What?" my lips whispered by themselves.

"Perhaps I might be allowed to see what his excellency is concealing in his right hand?"

"Not possible," I whispered. But suddenly even the soles of my feet felt cold.

"Even this is not possible?"

"I can't, Daddy."

"His highness is showing us no favor today," Father summed up, sadly. Yet, despite everything, condescended to keep on pressing me: "For my benefit. And yours. For both our benefits."

"I can't."

"You will show me, you stupid child," roared Father. At that moment, my stomach began to hurt me dreadfully.

"I've got a tummy ache," I said.

"First you're going to show me what you've got in your hand."

"Afterwards," I begged.

"All right," said Father, in a different tone of voice. And repeated suddenly, "All right. That's enough." And moved out of the doorway. I looked up at him, hoping above hope that he was going to forgive me after all. And in that very moment came the first of the slaps.

And the second. And afterwards the third. But, by then, I'd ducked out of the way of his hand and run outside into the street, running as hard as I could, bent low from sheer fright, just like Goel's dog when he ran away from me. I was in tears almost; in the process of making the dreadful decision: that I would shake the dust of that house from my feet forever. And not just of the house; of the whole neighborhood, of Jerusalem. Now, at this moment, I'd set out on a journey from which I'd never return. Not forever and ever.

So my journey began; but, instead of heading directly for Africa, as I'd planned earlier, I turned east, towards Geula Street, in the direction of Mea Shearim; from there I'd cross the Kidron Valley and follow the Mount of Olives road into the Judean Desert and thence to the Jordan crossing and thence to the Mountains of Moab, and on and on and on.

Ever since I was in Class Three or Four, my imagination had been captured by the Himalaya Mountains, those sublime ranges at the heart of Asia. "There," I'd once read in an encyclopedia, "there, among them, rears the highest mountain in the world, its peak as yet unsullied by the foot of man." And there too, among those remote mountains, roamed that mysterious creature, the Abominable Snowman, scouring god-forsaken ravines for his prey. The very words filled me with dread and enchantment:

   ranges
      roams
         ravines
           remote
              sublime, unsullied,
                eternal snows
                   and distant peaks.

And, above all, that marvelous word: Himalaya. On cold nights, lying beneath my warm winter blanket, I would repeat it over and over, in the deepest, most reverberant voice I could drag from the depths of my lungs, Hi—ma—la—ya.

If I could only climb to the heights of the Moab Mountains, I would look east and see far away the snow-capped peaks that were the Himalayas. And then, I would leave the land of Moab and travel south through the Arabian Desert, across the Gate of Tears to the coast of the Horn of Africa. And I would penetrate the heart of the jungle to the source of the River Zambezi, in the land of Obangi-Shari. And there, all alone, I'd live a life that was wild and free.

So, desperate, and burning with eagerness, I made my way east up Geula Street to the corner of Chancellor Street. But, when I reached Mr. Bialig's grocery, one thought overcame the rest; persistent, merciless, it repeated over and over. Crazy boy, crazy boy, crazy boy. Really you are crazy, stark raving mad, bad as Uncle Wetmark, maybe even worse; for all you know you'll grow up a *spekulant,* just like him. And what exactly did the word *spekulant* mean? I still did not know.

And suddenly all the pain and humiliation seemed to well up inside me, until I could scarcely bear it. The darkness was complete now in Geula Street. Not the darkness of early evening, full of children's cries and mothers' scoldings; this was the chill and silent darkness of the night, better seen from indoors, from your bed, through a crack in the shutters. You did not want to be caught out in it alone. Very occasionally someone else came hurrying by. Mrs. Soskin recognized me and asked what was the matter. But I did not answer her a word. From time to time a British armored car from the Schneller Barracks charged past at a mad gallop. I would seek out Sergeant Dunlop, walking his poodle in Haturim Street or Tahkemoni Street, I thought, and this time I would give him information after all; I'd tell him it was Goel Germanski who painted that slogan against the High Commissioner. And then I would go to London and turn double agent. I'd kidnap the King of England and say to the English Government straight out: "Give us back the land of Israel and I'll give you back your King. Don't give, don't get." (And even this idea came from my Uncle Zemach.) There, sitting on the steps of Mr. Bialig's grocery, I rehearsed all the details of my plan. It was late now; the hour the heroes of the Underground emerged from their hiding places, while around them, detectives and informers and tracker dogs lay in wait.

I was on my own. Aldo had taken my bicycle away and made me sign a contract to say so. Goel had expropriated my marvelous railway and the tame wolf roamed the woods and forests without me. And I was never to set foot in my parents' house again, not forever and forever. Esthie hated me. The despicable Aldo had stolen my notebook full of poems and sold it to that hoodlum Goel.

Then what was left? Just the pencil sharpener, nothing else. And what could I get from a pencil sharpener; what

good could it do me? None. All the same, I'd keep it forever
and ever. I swore an oath that I would keep it, that no
power on earth would take it from my hand.

So I sat at nine o'clock at night—or even at a quarter
past nine—on the steps of Mr. Bialig's shuttered grocery
shop and wept, almost. And so too I was found by a tall
and taciturn man who came walking along the deserted
street, smoking, peacefully, a pipe with a silver lid; Esthie's
father, Mr. Engineer Inbar.

"Oh," he said, after he had leaned down and seen me.
"Oh. It is you. Well, well. Is there anything I can do to
help?"

It seemed beautiful to me, miraculous even, that
Engineer Inbar should speak to me like that, as one adult to
another, without a trace of that special kind of language
and tone of voice that people use to children.

"Can I help you in any way?" I might have been a driver
whose car had broken down, struggling to change a tire in
the dark.

"Thanks," I said.

"What's the problem?" asked Engineer Inbar.

"Nothing," I said. "Everything's fine."

"But you're crying. Almost."

"No. No, not at all. I'm not crying. Almost. I'm just a bit
cold. Honestly."

"All right. We're not going the same way by any chance?
Are you on your way home too?"

"Well . . . I haven't got a home."

"How do you mean?"

"I mean . . . my parents are away in Tel Aviv. They're coming back tomorrow. They left me some food in the icebox. I mean . . . I had a key on a piece of white string."

"Well, well. I see. You've lost your key. And you've got nowhere to go. That's it in a nutshell. Exactly the same thing happened to me when I was still a student in Berlin. Come on then. Let's go. There's no point in sitting here all night, weeping. Almost."

"But . . . where are we going?"

"Home. Of course. To our place. You can stay the night with us. There's a sofa in the living room, also a camp bed somewhere. And I'm sure Esthie will be glad. Come on. Let's go."

And how my foolish heart ran wild; it beat inside my T-shirt, inside my vest, inside my skin and bone. Esthie will be glad—oh, Esthie will be glad.

> *Pomegranate scents waft to and fro*
> *From the Dead Sea to Jericho.*

Esthie will be glad.

I must never lose it; my pencil sharpener, my perfect, lucky pencil sharpener that I held in my hand that I held inside my pocket.

## ONE NIGHT OF LOVE

*How only he who has lost everything may sue for happiness.*
*"If a man offered for love all the wealth of his house . . ."*
*And how we were not ashamed.*

So there we sat at supper together, the Engineer Inbar and I, discussing the state of the country. Esthie's elder brother was away building a new kibbutz at Beit She'an, while her mother must have eaten before we came. Now she set before us on a wooden dish slices of some peculiar bread, very black and strong-tasting, together with Arab cheese, very salty, and scattered with little cubes of garlic. I was hungry. Afterwards we ate whole radishes, red outside, white and juicy inside. We chewed big lettuce leaves. We drank warm goat's milk. (At our house, that is to say the house that used to be mine, I'd get a poached egg in the evening, with tomato and cucumber, or else boiled fish, and afterwards yogurt and cocoa. My father and mother ate the same, except they finished up with tea instead of cocoa.)

Mrs. Inbar gathered up the plates and cups and went back to the kitchen to prepare lunch for the next day. "Now we'll leave the men to talk men's talk," she said. Mr. Engineer Inbar pulled off his shoes and put his feet up on a small stool. He lit his pipe carefully, and said, "Yes. Very good."

And I tightened my fingers round the pencil sharpener in my pocket and said, "Thank you very much."

And afterwards we exchanged opinions on matters of politics. Him in his armchair; me on the sofa.

The light came from a lamp the shape of a street lamp on a copper column, which stood in one corner beside the desk and between one wall covered in books and maps and another hung with pipes and mementoes. A huge globe stood in the room too, on a pedestal. At the slightest touch of a finger I thought it could be made to spin round and round. I could hardly take my eyes off it.

All this time Esthie remained in the bathroom. She did not come out. There was only the sound of running water sometimes from behind the locked door at the end of the corridor, and sometimes, also, Esthie's voice singing one of the popular songs of Shoshana Damari.

"The Bible," said Engineer Inbar amid his cloud of smoke, "the Bible, quite right, no doubt, of course. The Bible promises us the whole land. But the Bible was written at one period, whereas we live in quite another."

"So what?" I cried, politely furious. "It makes no difference. Perhaps the Arabs called themselves Jebusites or Canaanites in those days, and the British were called Philistines. But so what? Our enemies may keep changing their masks, but they keep persecuting us just the same. All our festivals prove it. The same enemies. The same wars. On and on, almost without a break."

Engineer Inbar was in no hurry to reply. He grasped his pipe and scratched the back of his neck with the stem. And afterwards, as if he found an answer difficult, he began gathering up from the table every stray crumb of tobacco and impounding them carefully in the ashtray.

248

When the operation was complete, he raised his voice and called:

"Esther! Perhaps it's time you made harbor and came to see who's waiting for you here. Yes. A visitor. A surprise. No, I'm not going to tell you who it is. Come to dry land quickly and you'll see for yourself. Yes. The Arabs and British. Certainly. Canaanites and Philistines, from the day that they were born. A very intriguing idea. Only you'll have to try and persuade them to see matters in the same light. The days of the Bible, alas, are over and done with. Ours are a different matter altogether. Who on earth nowadays can turn walking sticks into crocodiles and beat rocks to make water come out? Look, I brought these sweets back last week, straight from Beirut, by train. Try one. Go on. Enjoy it. Don't be afraid. It's called *Rakhat Lokoom*.* Eat up. Isn't it sweet and tasty? And you—I assume you belong to some political party already?"

"Me? Yes," I stammered. "But not like Father . . . the opposite . . ."

"Then you support the activities of the Underground absolutely and resist any suggestion of compromise," stated Engineer Inbar, without a question mark. "Very good. Then we are of different minds. By the way, your school satchel with all your books and exercise books must be locked up at home in your flat. That's a pity. You'll have to go to school tomorrow with Esthie, but without your

---

* **Rakhat Lokoom.** Turkish Delight. —*Trans.*

satchel. Esther! Have you drowned in there? Perhaps we'd
better throw you a life belt or something."

"Please could I have another piece?" I asked politely; and
boldly, not waiting for a reply, pulled nearer to me the jar
of *Rakhat Lokoom*. It really was delicious, even if it did
come straight from the city of Beirut.

It was so good to sit here in this room, behind closed
shutters, and between the walls covered in books and maps
and the wall hung with pipes and mementoes, immersed
in frank men's talk with Engineer Inbar. It seemed miraculous that Engineer Inbar did not snub or ridicule me, did
not talk down, merely remarked, "Then we are of different
minds"—how I loved that expression "We are of different
minds." And I loved Esthie's father almost as much as I
loved Esthie, only in a different way; perhaps I loved him
more. It began to seem possible to open my heart and confess just how badly I'd lied to him; to make a clean breast of
today's shame and disgrace, not even keeping from him
where I was journeying to and the roads I intended to take.
But, just then, at last, Esthie emerged from the bathroom. I
almost regretted it—this interruption to our frank men's
talk. Her hair was not in its plaits now—instead, there fell
to her shoulders a newly-washed blonde mane, still warm
and damp, still almost steaming. And she wore pajamas
with elephants all over them, large and small ones in different colors; on her feet her mother's slippers, much too big
for her. She threw a quick glance at me as she came in, then
went straight over to where her father, Engineer Inbar, was
sitting. I might have been yesterday's newspapers left lying

on the sofa; or else I stopped there every evening on my way to the land of Obangi-Shari, there was nothing whatever in it.

"Did you go to Jericho today?" Esthie asked her father.

"I did."

"Did you buy me what I asked?"

"I didn't."

"It was too expensive?"

"That's right."

"Will you look again for me when you're in Bethlehem next?"

"Yes."

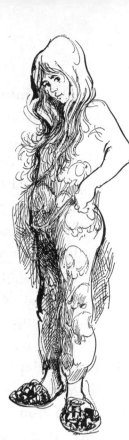

"And was it you brought him here?"

"Yes."

"What's it all about then? What's up with him?"

(I still didn't merit one word, one glance from Esthie. So I kept silent.)

"His parents are away and he lost his key. Exactly the same thing happened to me when I was a student in Berlin. We bumped into each other on Geula Street and I suggested he come to us. Mummy has already given him something to eat. He can spend the night on the sofa in the living room, or else on the camp bed, in your room. It's up to you."

Now, all at once, suddenly, Esthie turned towards me. But still without looking at me directly.

"Do you want to sleep in my room? Will you promise to tell me crazy stories before we go to sleep?"

251

"Don't mind," muttered my lips, quite of their own volition because I was still too stunned.

"What did he say?" Esthie asked her father a little anxiously. "Perhaps you heard what he said?"

"It seemed to me," answered Engineer Inbar, "it seemed to me that he was still weighing up the possibilities."

"Weighing-schneighing," laughed Esthie. "OK, that's it, let him sleep in here, in the living room and be done with it. Good night."

"But Esthie," I succeeded in saying at last, if still in a whisper only, "But Esthie . . ."

"Good night," said Esthie, and went out past me in her cotton elephant pajamas, the smell of her damp hair lingering behind her. "Good night, Daddy."

And from outside in the passage, she said, "Good. My room then. I don't mind."

Who ever, before, saw a girl's room, late, towards bedtime, when the only light burns beside her bed. Oh yes, even a girl's room has walls and windows, a floor and a ceiling, furniture and a door. That's a fact. And yet, for all that, it feels like a foreign country, utterly other and strange, its inhabitants not like us in any way. For instance: there are no cartridge cases on the windowsill, no muddy gym shoes buried under the bed. No piles of rope, metal, horseshoes, dusty books, pistol caps, padlocks, and India rubber bands; no spinning tops, no strips of film. Nor are there subversive pamphlets from the Underground hidden between the cupboard and the wall and, presumably, no dirty pictures concealed among the pages of her geography book. And there aren't, wouldn't ever be in a girl's room, any empty beer cans, cats' skulls, screwdrivers, nails, springs and cogs and hands from dismantled watches, penknife blades, or drawings of blazing battleships pinned up along the wall.

On the contrary.

In Esthie's room, the light was almost a color in itself; warm, russet-colored light, from the bedside lamp under its red raffia lampshade. Drawn across its two windows were the blue curtains that I'd seen a thousand times from the other side, and never dreamed I'd see from this, all the days of my life. On the floor was a small mat made of plaited straw. There was a white cupboard with two brown drawers in it, and, in the shadowy gap between wall and cupboard, a small, very tidy desk on which I could see Esthie's schoolbooks, pencils, and paintbox. A low bed, already turned down for sleep, stood between the two windows; a folded counterpane, the color of red wine, at its head. Another camp bed had been placed ready for me, as close as possible to the door.

In one corner, on a stool covered with a cloth, there nestled a tall jug filled with pine branches and a stork made out of a pine cone and chips of colored wood. There were two more chairs in the room. One of them I could scarcely take my eyes off. But the bedside lamp bestowed its quiet light on everything alike. Russet-colored light. You are in a girl's room, I thought. In Esthie's room, I thought. And you just sit and don't say anything because you are just a great big dummy. That sums it up, Soumchi, absolutely sums it up. Which thought is not going to help me find the right words for starting a conversation. With much agony, I

253

managed to squeeze out the following sentence, more or less:

"My room, at home, is quite different from this."

Esthie said, "Of course. But now you're here, not there."

"Yes," I said, because it was true.

"What do you keep staring at all the time?" asked Esthie

"Nothing in particular," I said. "I'm just sitting here . . . just sitting. Not looking at anything in particular." That, of course, was a lie. I could scarcely take my eyes off the arms of the second chair on which she'd laid the beloved white jumper, the very same jumper that, at school, I'd stuck time and again to the seat of her chair with chewing gum. Oh, God, I thought. Oh, God, why did you make me such an idiot? Why was I ever born? At this moment it would be better not to exist. Not anywhere. Not anywhere at all, except perhaps in the Himalaya Mountains or the land of Obangi-Shari, and even there they don't need such an idiot as me.

And so it was, after scraping those few words together, I sat dumb again on the folding bed in Esthie's room, my right hand still gripped tightly round my pencil sharpener and sweating a little in my pocket.

Esthie said, "Perhaps, after all, you'd rather sleep in the living room."

"It doesn't matter," I whispered.

"What doesn't matter?"

"Nothing. Really."

"OK. If that's what you want. I'm getting into bed now and I'm going to turn round to the wall until you've got yourself quite settled."

But I did not think of settling myself quite. Still fully dressed in my very short gym shorts and Hasmonean T-shirt, I lay under the light blanket, taking nothing off but my gym shoes which I threw as deep as possible beneath the bed.

"That's it. All clear."

"If you want, now you can tell me about the mutiny of the great Mahdi in the Sudan, just like you did to Ra'anana and Nourit and all the rest of them the day Mr. Shitrit was ill and we had two free periods."

"But you didn't want to listen then."

"But now is not then. It's now," Esthie pointed out quite correctly.

"And if you didn't listen to the story, how do you know that it was about the rebellion of the Mahdi in the Sudan?"

"I do know. Generally I know everything."

"Everything?"

"Everything about you. Perhaps even the things you think I don't know."

"But there's one thing you don't know and I won't ever tell you," I said, very quickly, in one breath and with my face to the wall and my back to Esthie.

"I do know."

"You don't."

"Yes."

"No."

"Yes."

"Then tell me and we'll see."

"No."

"That means you're only saying you know. You don't

know anything."

"I know. And how."

"Then tell me. Now. And I swear I'll tell you if you're right."

"You won't tell."

"I swear I'll tell."

"Good then. It's this. That you love some girl in our class."

"That's rubbish. Absolutely."

"And you wrote her a love poem."

"You're nuts. You're mad. Stop it!"

"In a black notebook."

I would steal a thermometer from the medicine cabinet, I decided there and then. And I would break it. And, at the ten o'clock break, I'd let the mercury run out and mix a little of it with Aldo's cocoa and a little with Goel Germanski's. So that they'd die. And also Bar-Kochba's and Elie's and Tarzan Bamberger's. So that they'll all be dead, once and for all.

Esthie repeated:

"In a little black notebook. Love poems. And also poems about how you'd run away with this girl to the Himalaya Mountains, or some place in Africa—I forget the name."

"Shut up, Esthie. Or I'll throttle you. This minute here. That's enough."

"Don't you love her anymore?"

"But it's all lies, Esthie. It's all lies invented by those bastards. I don't love any girl."

"Good," said Esthie, and all at once turned out her

bedside light. "That's OK. If that's how you want it. Now go to sleep. I don't love you either."

And afterwards, while the street light slid through the cracks in the shutters and painted the room with stripes, on the table and on the chairs, on the cupboard and on the floor, on Esthie herself in her elephant pajamas, lying at the other end of the straw mat at the foot of my bed, we talked a little more. In a whisper, I confessed almost everything. About Uncle Zemach and me; about how I was like him, a crazy boy, and for all anyone knew, a *spekulant* too in the end; about what it felt like to get up and leave everything, to go in search of the source of the River Zambezi in the land of Obangi-Shari. About how I'd left all of it, the house, the neighborhood, the city, and how, in one day, I'd managed to lose a bicycle, an electric railway, a dog, and even my own home. How I'd been left without anything, except the pencil sharpener I found. Till late, very late at night, perhaps about eleven o'clock, I went on whispering to Esthie and she listened to me without a single word. But then, during the silence that fell, when I'd finished my story, she said, very suddenly:

"Good. Now give me this pencil sharpener."

"The pencil sharpener? Why give you the pencil sharpener?"

"Never mind. Give it me."

"Here you are then. Will you love me now?"

"No. And now be quiet."

"Then why are you touching my knee?"

"Will you be quiet. Why does he always have to say

things and make trouble? Don't say any more."

"OK." I said. But was forced to add, "Esthie."

Esthie said, "Enough. Don't say another word. I'm going away now to sleep on the sofa in the living room. Don't say anything. And don't say anything tomorrow either. Good night. And anyway, there's no such place as the land of Obangi-Shari. But it's marvelous all the same that you've invented a place for just us two alone. Goodbye, then, till tomorrow."

For six weeks Esthie and I were friends. All those days were blue and warm and the nights were blue and dark. It was full, deep summer in Jerusalem while we loved each other, Esthie and I.

To the end of the school year, our love continued, and a little after, over the summer holidays. What names our class called us, what stories they told, what a joke they found it. But all the time we loved each other, nothing could worry us. Then our friendship was over and we parted, I won't say on account of what. Haven't I already written, in the prologue, how time keeps on passing and that the whole world changes? In fact, this brings me to the end of my story. In a single sentence I can tell you all of it. How once I was given a bicycle and swapped it for a railway; got a dog instead; found a pencil sharpener in place of the dog and gave the pencil sharpener away for love. And even this is not quite the truth, because the love was there all the time, before I gave the sharpener away, before these exchangings began.

Why did love cease? That is just one question. But there

are many other questions I could ask if I wanted. Why did that summer pass, and the summer after? And another summer and another and another? Why did Engineer Inbar fall ill? Why does everything change in the world? And why, since we happen to be asking questions, why, now that I'm grown up, am I still here and not among the Himalaya Mountains and not in the land of Obangi-Shari?

Well then; but there are so many questions and among them some so very hard to answer. But, as for me, I've reached the end of my story—so, if anyone else can provide us with the answers, let him rise to his feet and give them to us now.

EPILOGUE

ALL'S WELL THAT ENDS WELL

*Which may be skipped altogether. I only wrote it because it is expected.*

At midnight, or perhaps just after midnight, Mother and Father arrived at the Inbar family house, looking pale and frightened. Father had been searching for me since half past nine. First he had gone to inquire for me at my Aunt Edna's in the Yegia Capiim neighborhood. Then he had returned to our own neighborhood and inquired equally vainly at Bar-Kochba's and Elie Weingarten's. At a quarter past ten he had arrived at Goel Germanski's; they had awoken Goel and interrogated him closely, Goel claiming that he knew absolutely nothing. By which Father's suspicions had been aroused; he had cross-examined Goel briefly himself, and, in the course of that, the agitated Goel swore several times that the dog did belong to him and that he even had a license from the city council to prove it. Father had dismissed him at last, saying "We are going to have another little chat some time, you and I," and continued his search through the neighborhood. But it was nearly midnight before he learned from Mrs. Soskin that I had been seen sitting on the steps of Mr. Bialig's grocery, in tears, almost, and that half an hour later, Mrs. Soskin had happened to peer through her north-facing shutter and seen me still sitting there, and then, "All of a sudden, Mr. Engineer Inbar had appeared and enticed the boy away with him, by kind words and promises."

His face very white, his voice very low and quiet, Father said:

"So, here's our jewel at last; asleep in his clothes, the crazy boy. Get up please, and kindly put on your sweater that your mother has been toting round for you all evening from house to house till twelve o'clock at night. We'll go straight home now, and leave all accounts to be settled tomorrow. Forward march!"

He made polite apologies to Engineer Inbar and his wife, thanked them and begged them in the morning to thank dear Esther also (whom, as we departed, I saw briefly a long way off through the open living room door. She was tossing from side to side in her sleep, disturbed by the voices and murmuring something, probably that it was all her fault and they should not punish me. But no one besides me heard and I did not really).

Back in my bed, at home, I lay all night awake and bright and happy until the crack of day. I did not sleep. I did not want to sleep. I saw the moon depart from my window and the first line of light start gleaming in the east. And, at last, the sun setting early sparkles on drainpipes and windowpanes, I said out loud, almost:

"Good morning, Esthie."

And indeed a new day was beginning. At breakfast, Father said to Mother, "All right. As you want. Let him grow up a Wetmark. I'll just keep my mouth shut."

Mother said, "If it's all the same to you, my brother's name is Zemach, not Wetmark."

Father said, "That's all right by me. Good. So be it."

At school, by the ten o'clock break, this had already appeared on the blackboard:

> *In the midnight, under the moon*
> *Soumchi and Esthie start to spoon.*

And the teacher, Mr. Shitrit, wiped it all off with a duster and calmly implored as follows:

"Not a dog shall bark. Let all flesh be silent."

On his return from work on that same day, at five o'clock, the turn of the evening, Father went alone to the Germanskis' house. He explained; apologized; made frank and complete statement of the facts; took possession of the electric railway and turned his footsteps, steadily and without haste, to the house of the Castelnuovo family. There, Louisa, the Armenian nanny, ushered him into

Professor Castelnuovo's aromatic library and Father made an impartial statement of the facts to Mrs. Castelnuovo in her turn. He apologized; received apologies; handed over the railway and took possession of the bicycle. And so, at last, everything was restored to its rightful place once more.

The bicycle itself, of course, was confiscated and locked up in the cellar for three months. But I have already written how, by the end of the summer, everything had changed; how nothing stayed the same as before. How other concerns took over. But they, perhaps, belong to some other story.

# ACKNOWLEDGMENTS

All possible care has been taken to trace ownership and secure permission for each selection in this series. The Great Books Foundation wishes to thank the following authors, publishers, and representatives for permission to reprint copyrighted material:

*Through the Tunnel,* from THE HABIT OF LOVING, by Doris Lessing. Copyright 1957 by Doris Lessing. Reprinted by permission of HarperCollins Publishers.

*Raymond's Run,* from GORILLA, MY LOVE, by Toni Cade Bambara. Copyright 1970 by Toni Cade Bambara. Reprinted by permission of Random House, Inc.

*My Greatest Ambition,* from OUTRAGEOUS BEHAVIOUR: BEST STORIES OF MORRIS LURIE. Copyright 1969, 1975, 1979, 1981 by Morris Lurie. Reprinted by permission of the author.

A LIKELY PLACE, by Paula Fox. Copyright 1967 by Paula Fox. Reprinted by permission of Macmillan Publishing Company.

*The Mysteries of the Cabala,* from A DAY OF PLEASURE, by Isaac Bashevis Singer. Copyright 1963, 1965, 1966, 1969 by Isaac Bashevis Singer. Reprinted by permission of Farrar, Straus and Giroux, Inc.

*Bad Characters,* from THE COLLECTED STORIES, by Jean Stafford. Copyright 1954, 1969 by Jean Stafford; renewed 1982 by Josephine Monsell. Reprinted by permission of Farrar, Straus and Giroux, Inc.

*Chura and Marwe,* from TALES TOLD TO AN AFRICAN KING, by Humphrey Harman. Copyright 1978 by Humphrey Harman. Reprinted by permission of Century Hutchinson Publishing Group Limited.

*Superstitions,* from HOUSE OF HEROES AND OTHER STORIES, by Mary La Chapelle. Copyright 1988 by Mary La Chapelle. Reprinted by permission of Crown Publishers, Inc.

*The Last Great Snake,* from THE OWL'S KISS, by Mary Q. Steele. Copyright 1978 by Mary Q. Steele. Reprinted by permission of William Morrow & Company, Inc.

*Gaston,* by William Saroyan. Copyright 1962 by The Atlantic Monthly Company; renewed 1990 by the William Saroyan Foundation. Reprinted by permission of the William Saroyan Foundation.

SOUMCHI, by Amos Oz. Copyright 1978 by Amos Oz and Am Oved Publishers Limited, Tel Aviv. Translation copyright 1980 by Chatto & Windus Limited. Reprinted by permission of Deborah Owen Limited.

# ILLUSTRATION CREDITS

Papas' illustrations for *Soumchi* are from the book of the same name. Illustrations copyright 1980 by Papas. Reprinted by permission of Century Hutchinson Publishing Group Limited.

Cover art by Ed Young. Copyright 1992 by Ed Young.

Text and cover design by William Seabright,
William Seabright & Associates.